LIVING HAPPILY EVER AFTER

*Toward a Theology
of Christian Marriage*

Thomas N. Hart

PAULIST PRESS
New York/Ramsey/Toronto

Excerpts from "i carry your heart" and "i am a birdcage without any bird" by e. e. cummings are taken from *Complete Poems 1913-1962* and used by permission of Harcourt Brace Jovanovich, Inc., publisher.

Library of Congress
Catalog Card Number: 79-89475

ISBN: 0-8091-2253-7

Published by Paulist Press
Editorial Office: 1865 Broadway, New York, N.Y. 10023
Business Office: 545 Island Road, Ramsey, N.J. 07446

Printed and bound in the
United States of America

CONTENTS

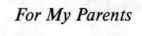

For My Parents

INTRODUCTION

Most Christians marry, and live out a married vocation the greater part of their lives. Yet Christian theology has produced very little in the way of theological reflection on marriage. There is a lot of material on the theology of priesthood, and even more on the theology of religious life. There are countless studies on prayer, and, fortunately, a growing number of them presume lay life and preoccupations rather than the relative isolation of the monastery. Yet most spiritual theology is written for those people, priests and religious, supposed to be uniquely interested in living a "spiritual life." Very little of it is addressed to married Christians whose vocation it is to devote themselves to the difficult business of loving one another truly and faithfully, bringing up their children in a proper environment, and doing all they can to make the marketplace more Christian. There are probably several reasons for this lack, but perhaps the greatest of them is that until very recently, at least in the Roman Catholic Church, theology has been the work of celibates. It has been done by celibates for celibates, and married concerns, being too much out of sight, have also been too much out of mind.

Married Christians have suffered the lack. They have also suffered its implication: that they are less important. And there have been sufficient confirmations. Priestly and religious

1

vocations have been highly exalted in the hearing of the people, and priests and religious have been so set apart in their mode of life and so much in charge in the Church that those who marry think of themselves as second-class Christians. They are made to feel that they have opted for the easier way, and are married by a kind of default, as a concession to human weakness. Sex in particular is such a concession. Then the "worldly cares" that follow on the choice to marry constitute a drag on the soul, militating against any real growth in Christian holiness. Only extraordinary heroism in this state of life, whatever that would be, could bring married people into approximation with the sort of sanctity which accrues to priests and religious just by reason of their state and way of life.

Sometimes those who are married aspire to a greater holiness, so they apprentice themselves to a priest or religious. The working presumption is that they will become holy in the measure that they can assimilate the life style of their mentor, since that is the way of Christian holiness. It will consist in setting aside a sizable portion of the day for personal prayer, participating daily or nearly so in the Eucharist, trying to find time to go apart for retreats and days of recollection, perhaps saying part of the Divine Office, maybe practicing a form of penance, finding an apostolate to which they can devote some time, and receiving regular spiritual direction. They try these things for a while, and the conviction deepens that they are second-class Christians. For, do what they may, they cannot garner the time priests and religious can for prayer, Eucharist, retreats, or apostolate, but remain inferior in all of these. Nor can they escape the incessant needs and demands of spouse and children, friends and neighbors, business, home, and school—in a word, all their "worldly cares." The point has been proved. They are second-class. Christian holiness lies down the other road, the road not taken.

It might be interesting to married people to know that

most priests and religious do not feel holy either (though some of them are), and that those who do are probably not. Priests and religious too feel that they devote insufficient time to prayer, and that the praying they do is of poor quality. They feel the littleness of their love of God and their lack of generosity in meeting the needs of needy neighbors. Their lives too are deadened by monotony and routine, lack of spirit and want of imagination. They often feel they have not left the world at all but are very much a part of it, and are weighed down with all the same pressing demands and "worldly cares" that everyone else shares. Their apostolic work is very limited in its scope, sometimes of questionable relevance to real human need, and often not very conspicuously fruitful. In short, they too feel mediocre, even though they are supposed to be the first-class Christians.

It is interesting in the face of all this experience that the Second Vatican Council moved to blur the distinction between first and second class Christians in the Church, built up over many centuries. It dropped the language of "wholeheartedness" as the distinguishing mark of those who choose celibate life, with its strong implication that those who do not are not wholehearted. The strongest expression Vatican II uses of celibates is that they might "more easily" or "more readily" devote themselves to things that need to be done (*Decree on Religious Life*, 1, 12), but it gives them no blanket advance on holiness. And in the *Dogmatic Constitution on the Church*, instead of beginning with the Church's hierarchical structure, which always seems to point up a sharp distinction between rulers and ruled, teachers and taught, sanctifiers and sanctified, it first describes the Church as the entire people of God, the whole Body of Christ. Only with these conceptual foundations securely in place does it descend to a description of how leadership is exercised within the Christian community. And then it moves back again to the whole people in the chapter entitled "The Universal Call to Holiness," here emphatically asserting that all God's people are called to the fullness of Christian sanctity and that that sanctity is available to all in and through all the more particular vocations within the large one (*Constitution on the Church*, 40). All Christians are likewise called to the exercise of the apostolate (*Decree on the Apostolate of the Laity*, 1).

These reflections set the stage for the present book, which attempts to articulate a theology and spirituality of marriage. It tries to answer such questions as these: What difference, if any, does it make that a marriage is qualified as Christian? Does the perspective of faith have anything to say to married people, either about their position in the Church or about possibilities for growth in holiness? Or does Christian marriage simply mean that the parties to it are baptized and that the wedding takes place in church?

This is not a how-to-do-it book. It does not offer counsels or techniques either for survival or for bliss in marriage. There is no question about the usefulness of such books, no doubt about the problems married people face and need help with. But there are already many such books to be had, and many counselors too. What we have much less of is a theological treatment of marriage, a study which situates it in the context of faith, points out where in married experience God is likely to be encountered, indicates how a person who wants to follow Christ might do so in the married state. This is what the present work attempts. It should in its own way contribute something to married stability, enrichment, and satisfaction.

We will first examine what it means to follow Christ, whether one follow him as lay person, priest, or religious. Then we will examine several theological notions which have an important bearing on Christian marriage—sacrament, revelation, grace, and the paschal mystery. We will attempt to give these concepts a contemporary formulation and to apply them specifically to the married situation. Next we will turn to the key New Testament text on marriage, the fifth chapter of

4

Ephesians, with its comparison of the love between husband and wife and the love between Christ and the Church, and draw out its implications for a married spirituality. This will prepare the way for a more particular consideration of three important areas of married life: sex, the raising of children, and participation in the mission of the Church. Our final chapter will probe the troublesome area of failure in marriage, and treat some of the options open to a Christian in dealing with it.

Chapter One
TO FOLLOW JESUS

Let us for the moment set aside the inherited two-class mentality which has long prevailed in the Church and see if we can discover something more primary, a spirituality basic to all Christian vocations. Let us go back to the beginnings, to Jesus of Nazareth, and see if we can uncover those larger values common to all Christian paths. Married life, on the one hand, and priestly and religious life, on the other, may prove to be but variant approaches to a deep and strong ideal held in common.

Adopting a Style

Jesus was a layman. He did not come from the priestly clan of Judaism, the Levites. Nor did he do the traditional priestly things—offer public sacrifices, lead public prayers, reside and serve at the temple. He wore no special garb and advocated none. He was not a scribe or a Pharisee, schooled carefully in the Law and busy with its details, a member of the religious establishment of his day by reason of schooling, camaraderie, common concerns, and the respect of the people. Jesus was an independent, a layman, and a man of the road; and his usual company was the most ordinary people in the world. He himself did not marry, for reasons which are never set forth, but the vast majority of his followers presumably did. Tradition tells us that all of the Twelve were married, with the possible exception of John. Which means, among other things, that the first Pope was a married man. For if Simon had a mother-in-law whom Jesus cured, Simon had a wife (Mk. 1:30).

Judging by many subsequent historical developments, one would think Jesus, layman though he was, must at least have been notably ascetical, that he took a dim view of ordinary human life and its natural unfolding, that he found sex a particularly distracting thing, that he led people away from human society into solitary places where God could better be found and served. Yet a study of the Gospels yields none of this sort of evidence. Jesus certainly does not make a strong pitch for fasting. He was challenged by his religious compatriots precisely because he and his disciples did not fast whereas the Baptist's and the Pharisees' disciples did (Mk. 2:18). It is fascinating that among his contemporaries, far from being seen as an ascetic, he had the reputation of being a glutton and a drunkard and too often in bad company (Lk. 7:34). In the first of his signs in the Gospel of John, he is at a wedding feast, and he blesses it with a rather copious supply of wine—six water jars, or approximately 180 gallons. One searches the Gospels in vain for the polemic against sex or marriage, or for an emphatic summons to celibacy and solitude. One finds instead rather different things. Where people go wrong sexually, they are forgiven at once, without any discussion. Think of Magdalen (Lk. 7), the woman taken in adultery (Jn. 8), the prodigal son (Lk. 15), or Jesus' statement that the prostitutes and tax collectors will enter the Kingdom of God, where many who thought it was theirs will be found outside (Mt. 21:31). There is in the Gospels no campaign on behalf of sexual abstinence or any clear indication that marriage is an inferior way of following in Jesus' way. There are no discourses in this spirit,

8

no parables; nor does Jesus anywhere call attention either to his own or his mother's virginity. The brief and rather enigmatic saying about those who make themselves eunuchs for the sake of the Kingdom (Mt. 19:12) evokes various exegetical opinions. A strong case has been made that this text is not a call to celibacy as a way of life at all, but, in its context of teaching about marriage, a counsel to those who marry and suffer infidelity on the part of a spouse. Jesus' suggestion is that instead of marrying again they choose rather to wait for the return of the unfaithful partner, as the prophet Hosea did in the Old Testament, in order to witness to the Lord's faithful love for his sinful people. The text ends with the line, "Let that person take it who can," which implies that the counsel is by no means universally enjoined. It is interesting too that the statement made to Jesus, "Lo, we have left everything and followed you," which evokes his promise of a hundredfold in this present time and eternal life in the age to come, is made by Peter on his own and the disciples' behalf, and almost all of them are married men (Mk. 10:28).

All of this is not to say that celibacy is not Christian, or that it is not a good way to live the Christian life. It is clearly both, and many are still called to it. It has been blessed by the Church, and shown its fruitfulness through centuries. But an investigation of the teaching of Jesus strongly suggests that it is not the only way or even the ordinary way of responding to the Gospel, and that Jesus laid very little emphasis on it. What he emphasizes is the importance of love, of trust in God, of prayerfulness, of forgiveness, of simplicity of life, of humility and generosity, of accepting the great gift of life and God's love for us and being always grateful. Celibacy has value, but it will not be sufficient to establish one in a superior class of Christians.

If Jesus was not an ascetic in the sense that he urged fasting and sexual abstinence for growth in the spirit, did he at least advocate withdrawal from ordinary society into places

9

where God could more easily be found? Here again the answer seems to be No. Before he begins his public life, we do find him in the desert for forty days, fasting and praying. And in the midst of his public life, we find him regularly withdrawing for prayer, early in the morning or late at night. But his is not a desert way of life, nor do we find him trying to found desert communities.

> I do not pray that you should take them out of the world, but that you should keep them from evil (Jn. 17:15).
>
> As you sent me into the world, so I have sent them into the world (Jn. 17:18).

Jesus accepts the human condition, embraces the world, affirms the material, the body, the family of humankind. He lives by far the greater number of his earthly years in small town ordinariness. His public life is lived very much in the midst of it all. His typical days are working days in almost constant contact with people, needy individuals, large crowds, the Twelve. Sometimes there is no leisure to take a meal (Mk. 6:31). On one occasion when the crowds were pressing about him, he sought some time apart with his friends, only to find a crowd waiting in the place to which they went (Mk. 6:34), and again he ministered to them. He would rise at dawn to pray, and even then be sought out by people who wanted to see him (Mk. 1:35). Such was his life.

And his spirituality was of a piece with his life. All the illustrations he uses in his teaching are drawn from the midst of the world—illustrations from kings, banquets, family life, law courts, planting and harvest, seasons, storms, night and day, children, journeys, war, business dealings, shepherds and flocks, birds and animals and plants, sun and rain. Many have noticed this and remarked what a superb teacher he was, drawing thus for illustrative material on things within the ordinary experiences of his audiences. But isn't there another factor at work in his choice of these particular images? Do they not issue spontaneously from his own contemplative vision of life, his deep insight into the ordinary, his capacity for finding God in all things? If so, then there is a great lesson for us his followers too. Maybe God really is in all things, all the ordinary things and happenings of everyday life, for us too to discover and respond to, so that contact with him does not require a going apart unless it be for the purpose of heightening our awareness of the depth dimension of our usual environment. Paul says, "In him we live and move and have our being" (Acts 17:28). If those who are clean of heart shall see God, undoubtedly Jesus perceived the Father's creative hand in all things—here his beauty, there his power, here again his gentleness, there his wisdom, here his law, there his judgment, here again a gift and sign of his care, there his providence, everywhere his truth, and in human beings above all his presence. So Jesus uses the illustrative material he does not just to point to truths in the beyond, but to share his vision of the beyond in our midst, the openness to transcendence of the whole creation.

And where especially does he find value in life? He finds it in human beings. He loves them as they are. And because he does they become something else. He is entirely devoted to them, and his days are spent in serving them, healing their diseases, freeing them from their inner demons, forgiving their sins, teaching them to cherish and make the most of the gift of human life.

And by what is he sustained? Partly by the return on his labors, by a sense of the good he is able to achieve, and by the love that comes to him from people because he first so unquestioningly loves them. And partly by his rootedness in the One who sent him, whom he calls Father, to whom he prays, whom he obeys in all his choices and trusts in all the happenings of his life. His spirituality is summed up in these things, and all of it is available to us. In fact, he calls us all to follow and imitate him, the Way, the Truth, the Life (Jn. 14:6).

Radicalizing and Simplifying the Law

It is a very complicated religious stage onto which Jesus walks. There is the usual religious stratification into various classes, according to more and less, and a rigidly defined way of pleasing God, a way which has been gradually built up over many generations and now confronts the newcomer as an immense body of legislation, prescribing the religious life down to its finest details. There is plenty of religious ritual about: feasts to be celebrated, sacrifices to be offered, sabbaths to be observed, fasts to be made, prayers to be recited, tithes to be given. Society abounds in conspicuously religious figures— priests, prophets, ascetics, interpreters of God's law. There are desert movements and excited messianic expectations. In brief, it is a very religious culture.

Jesus cuts through it all. He simplifies and radicalizes the whole thing.

And one of the scribes came up and heard them disputing with one another, and seeing that he answered them well, asked him, "Which commandment is the first of all?" Jesus answered, "The first is, 'Hear, O Israel: The Lord our God, the Lord is one; and you shall love the Lord your God with all your heart, and with all your soul, and with all your mind, and with all your strength.' The second is this, 'You shall love your neighbor as yourself.' There is no other commandment greater than these." And the scribe said to him, "You are right, Teacher; you have truly said that he is one, and there is no other but he; and to love him with all the heart, and with all the understanding, and with all the strength, and to love one's neighbor as oneself is much more than all whole-burnt offerings and sacrifices." And when Jesus saw that he answered wisely,

12

he said to him, "You are not far from the kingdom of God." And after that no one dared to ask him any question (Mk. 12:28-34).

His radicalizing of the Law means his going to the root of it all, and stating quite plainly that God wants our hearts, not our external actions. He does not attend to each particular act, weighing its positive or negative value. It is the direction of our hearts that interests him, whether they are oriented and open to him or not in that by-and-large way which is the best the struggling human being can manage. Jesus' radicalizing of the Law is most clearly observable in the Sermon on the Mount (Mt. 5), where in a series of antitheses, "You have heard it said, but I say . . . ," he goes below the surface of external observance and articulates God's demand of total love. It is not enough not to kill according to the commandment; we must not vent anger on others. It is not enough not to commit adultery according to the commandment; the personhood of the other must always be reverenced. Swearing carefully according to certain conditions should be replaced by truth-telling as a way of life. It is not enough to love those who love us; we must love enemies, persecutors, and revilers too. In other words, no laws can cover what God really wants of us. He wants our hearts and the expression of our love of him in our love of neighbor.

This radicalization is also simplification. Jesus summarizes all Old Testament legislation, and all that a dozen and a half prophets have said over hundreds of years, in one single commandment: Love God with your whole heart and your neighbor as yourself. This commandment he himself lives so perfectly as to be for all time the supreme exemplar of it. And he names it the entire criterion by which God shall judge human beings at the end of the world (Mt. 25). For in Matthew's last judgment scene, God's question is not, "Were you validly baptized?" Or, "Were you regular in your Sunday

13

liturgy attendance?" Or, "Was your faith orthodox in every respect?" The question is rather, "What did you do when you saw your neighbor in need?" This is how God wants to be served, and he accepts it as service when no explicitly spiritual motive is operative.

> Then the righteous will answer him, "Lord, when did we see you hungry and feed you, etc.?" And the King will answer them, "Truly, I say to you, as you did it to one of the least of these my brothers and sisters, you did it to me" (Mt. 25:37-40).

Thus the righteous may not have seen the full spiritual significance of actions they took instinctively in response to human need, but the move to neighbor is one with the move to God, for in Christ God has identified himself with us all.

It is almost too simple. It is appallingly close to home. Yet it is the heart of the matter. And with that simple commandment, and the example of his own life, Jesus gives us his Spirit and missions us to do as he did. And now it is ours, in the same freedom and with the same generosity, to figure out in the particular situations of our lives what love calls for. In place of laws, Jesus gives us his own Spirit. It is at once freedom, discernment, and power.

The Trap

Something is there in the human being which will find this ordinariness unsatisfactory from time to time. The temptation will arise again and again, as it has through all of human religious history, to say this is not enough. And then legalism will be reborn and will attempt to set down exactly what the love and service of God demand in all the details of life, and again we will have a program. Or the elitist spirit will rise again, and various religious clubs will be formed, marked by a sense of superiority and self-righteousness, and exalting a particular path into *the* path for any who would serve God. The spirit of asceticism will wax anew, and fasting, corporal penance, long prayers, and love of the cross, preferably in places set apart, will replace the Lord's affirmation of life and the body and human beings in the celebration of love and community. All these temptations will arise from our restlessness, because restless we are on our pilgrim journey home. They will spring from a desire to feel holy and close to God, because we too seldom feel either. They will appeal because the simpler and more obvious things the Lord does clearly ask of us are very hard to give, and even in their performance do not usually yield us a sense that we have truly acquitted ourselves. But if we give in to these temptations, we will recreate the entire religious stage Jesus cleared with a whip of small cords. Would it not be better simply, humbly, and gratefully to accept the human condition, along with our sinfulness, living openly to the Lord and to one another as far as we can, yet always with the honest realization:

> So you also, when you have done all that is commanded you, say, "We are unworthy servants; we have only done what was our duty" (Lk. 17:10).

Can anything be saved from this perennially recurring extraordinary quest of holiness? Yes. From legalism, a respect for law, which does enshrine and try to protect value. From religious clubs, insight into the need for groups of people of like mind to share faith and hope and keep our vulnerable individuality on the path to life. From those who seek solitary places, the need we all have to withdraw now and then from the hurly-burly to be quiet and reflect before God on where we are going. From the ascetics, the truth that this world is not our final resting place and we should live in it simply rather than devote our energies to amassing treasure or consuming

15

everything we can. And from lovers of the cross, a willingness to suffer, after the example of Jesus, all the pain that genuine love and bearing witness to the truth will require of us.

The way of life Jesus sets before us cuts across all distinctions of status, and puts us all on the same footing before the same immense challenge. One might live it as a single person, a religious, a married person, a priest. Each way has its peculiar strengths and weaknesses. None is objectively superior to the others. The question any given individual must answer is: Which path best suits me? How do I feel called? For each of the ways is a genuine Christian vocation.

Suggestions for Further Reading

Quentin Quesnell, "Made Themselves Eunuchs for the Kingdom of God," in *Catholic Biblical Quarterly*, XXX, 3 (July, '68), 335-58.
Rudolph Bultmann, *Jesus and the Word*.

Chapter Two

THE CHURCH AS SACRAMENT

Having studied the main accents of a Christian spirituality, let us take a look at marriage as a Christian way of life, Christianity has always viewed marriage both as vocation and as sacrament. Its vocational aspects have already been adverted to. It is a specific modality of the general call to follow Christ, in living his way of life and continuing his work in the world. It is a particular focusing of the general command to love one's neighbor as oneself. And those persons are called to it who feel attracted to it, whose life-circumstances open onto it, who have a feeling of rightness about a lifetime commitment to a particular man or woman as the proper framework of their Christian commitment. We turn then to the sacramental nature of this way of life. What do we mean when we say marriage is a sacrament?

Roman Catholics have been raised on the notion that a sacrament is a visible sign of an invisible reality, or, closer to the formula classically employed, an outward sign instituted by Christ to give grace. There are seven such signs. Each bestows the grace that it signifies. Thus baptism gives the grace of Christian initiation by uniting the prospective Christian, in the presence of the community, with the death and resurrection of Christ, through the symbolism of going down into water and being drawn out again. The Eucharist gives the grace of a deeper union with Christ and with the members of his Body through participation together in a meal commemorating Christ's self-gift to the Father and to us in his death and resurrection. The sacrament of reconciliation makes visible, audible, and sometimes even tangible the reconciliation which Christ and his community extend to the sinner through the mediation of an ordained representative. These and the other sacraments are all visible signs of invisible realities. They bring God and his action on our behalf forcibly to recognition.

Contemporary theology, in consultation with the early Church Fathers, has broadened the notion of sacrament to embrace not only these seven signs, but the more primordial realities of Christ himself and the Church. In other words, there are two more basic levels of sacramentality than the level of the seven ritual sacraments. Christ is himself a sacrament, the primordial sacrament. And the Church is a sacrament too. From these the seven ritual actions of the Church derive their sacramentality.

In what sense is Christ a sacrament? He is surely the visible sign of an invisible reality. He incarnates the love of God for all humanity, and in incarnating it makes it known. It is to this that the prologue of the Fourth Gospel refers when it says: "No one has seen the Father; the only-begotten Son who lives in the bosom of the Father, he has made him known" (Jn. 1:18). This is the burden of Jesus' remark to Philip: "The person who has seen me has seen the Father" (Jn. 14:9). So whether we say Jesus is the incarnation of God, the revelation of God, or the sacrament of God, we are saying the same thing. And it is a tremendous thing. For God is a great mystery to us, and deeply involved in the mystery we call life. Things that happen to us, and the way this world goes, cause us to puzzle over God, to wonder at times whether there really is a God, and to wonder, if there is, what his attitudes toward us might be. Does he care? Is he angry? Vengeful? Malevolent? Capricious? It is because of questions like these which recur in our lives that we need the sacrament God has given us in Christ. That is, we need the revelation of the invisible. We need to revert back to the image of God we have in Jesus, the Jesus of the Gospels, so that we can rediscover the God before whom we live, know his attitudes toward us, understand how he deals with us and our world in our sinfulness and brokenness. Jesus is the primordial sacrament. For "He is the image of the invisible God, the first-born of all creation" (Col. 1:15). And "In him all the fullness of God was pleased to dwell" (Col. 1:19).

The Church

But is it only in the Gospels that we encounter him? Fortunately not. Otherwise a great many people would never encounter him at all. The fact is, we meet him also in the Church, for the Church is his sacrament. This needs to be understood. It does not mean that we encounter him whenever we walk into a church building, preferably when some sacramental action is taking place. The Church is not primarily a place. Nor is it primarily a hierarchy or a priesthood. Nor is it primarily ritual action. The Church is people, God's people, the whole Body of Christ. So just as Christ is the sacrament of God, the Church is the sacrament of Christ. That is, those who belong to Christ and who live in the world today are the incarnation or revelation of what is now invisible, the risen Christ.

It was the Second Vatican Council that officially endorsed this notion of the Church, gradually rehabilitated by contemporary theology. There was a movement away from a juridical understanding toward a more societal or communal understanding. Where the stress for some centuries had been

19

on the Church's organization, Pope, bishops, priests, people, and on the powers possessed by the hierarchy to teach, govern, and sanctify authoritatively in Christ's name, Vatican II recovered the biblical notion of the Church as the community of believers, the People of God, the Body of Christ, the Kingdom of God developing in the world. This return to biblical foundations has the decided advantage over the formulations which had arisen in recent history that it breaks down the we/they dichotomy which is still, even in the wake of the Council, the too prevalent mentality. On the juridical view, there are givers and receivers in the Church, teachers and learners, rulers and ruled, sanctifiers and sanctified. At worst, the conception is that there are some who *are* the Church (a small elite) and some who *belong* to the Church (the vast majority). That was what Vatican II was working against when it pulled away from this overstress on authority and organization and returned to principles which describe far more basically the reality of the Church. Those who believe in Christ and follow him are the Church, those who have received the gifts of the Holy Spirit by reason of their incorporation into his Body, those who are, all of them without exception and each in his or her own way, called to the fullness of Christian life. What all Christians have in common, membership in the Body of Christ, is surely more primary than their differentiation into various roles within that Body. And what most needs to be kept in mind about the Church is that it is people, not a building or buildings, not a hierarchy or priesthood, not a body of doctrines and a collection of rituals. The Church is Christians, and every statement about it should be a statement about Christians. That is the vision of the Second Vatican Council. Actually it is an ancient vision. It comes from the New Testament.

> For just as the body is one and has many members, and all
> the members of the body, though many, are one body, so

it is with Christ. For by one Spirit we were all baptized into one body (1 Cor. 12:12-13).

He is the head of the Body, the Church (Col. 1:18).

I am the Vine, you are the branches (Jn. 15:5).

When Vatican II calls the Church a sacrament, then, the statement means, on principles already developed, that Christians make something visible which would otherwise be invisible. And that something is Christ. Christians, in their lives, which, of course, extend far beyond those moments when they gather together for sacramental action, are a revelation of God to people. What does this mean? It means that just as Jesus could say, "The person who sees me sees the Father," Christians, when they really are Christians, can say, "The person who sees me, or, more fully, sees all of us, sees Christ."

The revelation of God thus made available to people through Christians has a double aspect. The first is that God's salvation, i.e., what his saving action accomplishes in human beings, is made manifest in what has happened to the people called Church. They are the recipients of a great grace, and have been transformed by it. In them people can see what their own (i.e., the world's) destiny is. For they model what the whole world is invited to be in the plan of God, what Jesus calls the Kingdom of God, begun on earth and completed in heaven.

And all who believed were together and had all things in common; and they sold their possessions and goods and distributed them to all, as any had need. And day by day, attending the temple together and breaking bread in their homes, they partook of food with glad and generous hearts, praising God and having favor with all the people. And the Lord added to their number day by day those who were being saved (Acts 2:44-47).

21

The second aspect of God's revelation through the Church is his attitude toward sinful human beings, made visible in Christians' attitudes toward sinful human beings. Through Christians, people can experience God's gracious outreach toward them. Vatican II strongly insists on the servant-model of the Church, the humble servant of the world, meeting men and women in all their temporal and spiritual needs as the incarnation of Jesus' own servant role. "For the Son of Man has come not to be served but to serve, and to give his life as a ransom for many" (Mk. 10:45).

In this twofold revelation, the Church fulfills its mission to the world. There is a popular saying which appears on banners: "You may be the only Bible some people ever read." That is very much to the point here. Many people will not only not read the Bible, they will not meet Christians in church either. And even those who do read the Bible and go to church, including Christians themselves, do not do these things most of the time. So the kind of modeling and serving we are talking about here must be done in ordinary everyday life, in office and factory, market and school, on the street and in the home. It is the full-time vocation of Christians as sacrament and revelation. The role of the seven ritual sacraments which Christ has given the Church is to renew and strengthen her for her task of being sacrament to the world.

Suggestions for Further Reading

Edward Schillebeeckx, *Christ the Sacrament of the Encounter with God*

Karl Rahner, *Church and Sacraments*

Juan Luis Segundo, *The Sacraments Today*

Vatican II, *Constitution on the Church, The Church in the Modern World*

Chapter Three

REVELATION, GRACE, AND THE PASCHAL MYSTERY TODAY

Besides the concept of sacrament, there are three other theological notions crucial to an understanding of Christian marriage. These are revelation, grace, and the paschal or passover mystery. In the present chapter we shall attempt to give them a contemporary presentation and apply them to married life.

Revelation

In classical theology, revelation is conceived as a deposit of truths. They were given to God's people in the Old Testament, and then to the Church over a period of time which ended with the death of the last apostle. They are now preserved and proclaimed by the Church and handed on from generation to generation. God has revealed to us what he wanted us to know, and we have only to look back to the record to read the truths he has disclosed.

Dynamically conceived, on the other hand, revelation has

rather a different aspect, and contemporary theology conceives it dynamically. On this view, what God reveals is not so much truths, but himself. That is, he offers himself to us for a relationship, and in that self-offering makes himself known. Thus what is revealed is not so much truths about God, but the living God himself, and this not just in the past but in the present and future as well, whenever and wherever anyone encounters him. We all do. In this way of viewing revelation, it is roughly the equivalent of religious experience.

What then do we have in the Bible and in that body of doctrines which constitute part of our tradition? They are the product of reflection on such encounters as we have described, verbal explicitations of rather more nameless experiences. In Karl Rahner's language, there is the transcendent experience itself, the encounter with the ineffable God, which he calls transcendental revelation. And there is the subsequent human formulation of it, which he calls categorical revelation, the human word which proceeds from human understanding, partly capturing and partly failing to capture the depth of the experience and its implications.

Perhaps the most profound consequence of this shift in perspective is that revelation is no longer so tied to past time. It is not so much that God revealed himself once upon a time, and the record of it is available to be read; but that God reveals himself now, in our day, again and again in various ways, always inviting us to relationship. The value of the inspired word, the Bible, is that it teaches us that God does disclose himself this way in human history, and has normatively shown himself to be the kind of God our common faith proclaims. This alerts us to be ready for such experiences of him as he may grace our history with. It also helps us distinguish genuine experiences of him from bogus ones, and true conclusions from false.

Now it is on such a notion of revelation that we have

based ourselves in speaking of marriage as sacrament and therefore as revelation. What we are claiming is that God reveals himself to a wife through her husband, and to a husband through his wife, and to others through them both, and thus he intrudes compellingly into our lives. In many other people and experiences too, of course, he reveals himself; we speak here of a privileged instance. Our spiritual growth, then, consists in becoming more aware of this presence and revelation, and more responsive to it. Such a spirituality keeps us squarely in the world, the arena of God's activity, for it is there that we encounter and make response to his mystery.

Grace

The theological notion of grace too has undergone a transformation. Formerly conceived, at least in its popular presentation, as some sort of mysterious quantity to be acquired and stored, it made us pleasing to God, empowered us to do certain things we could not otherwise do, and in its accumulation gave us a claim to heaven. You either had it or you did not, and that made all the difference.

The contemporary presentation of grace stresses an aspect of it which was present in earlier thought but less accented, namely, that grace is not primarily something which God gives us, but is rather something in God, his graciousness. God always acts graciously toward us, and this has the effect of making us gracious too. The graciousness of God is his love, and, like the love of a parent for a child, God's love for us gradually works a transformation such that we ourselves move from unloving to loving and from unlovable to lovable. Under its influence, we grow to the fullness of the personhood God intends for us. The process involves liberation, integration, development.

In other words, grace simply works the way love works.

It should not be reified, because it is not a thing. In God, where it is first found, it is a quality of graciousness toward us. Classical theology called this "uncreated grace." In us too it is a quality of graciousness, wrought by his faithful and careful love of us. Classical theology called this "created grace," a term which is accurate as long as it is understood that grace is not a separate entity which God bestows on us, but rather the created effect in us of his gracious loving.

We all know what love can do. In the fairy tales, the kiss of the prince awakens the princess from her sleep. In *Beauty and the Beast*, the beast is changed from beast to handsome prince because Beauty loves him. In *Man of LaMancha*, Dulcinea becomes a new creation under the sway of the same gentle power. In our own lives, we know what dramatic effects being loved can have, how it puts joy in our hearts and lightness in our step, generates a new hopefulness and an unaccustomed delight in being ourselves, and gives us fresh energy for loving other people.

In our relationship with God too, the world is recreated for us on the day when we experience his love and believe in it. This is the experience of grace. It sets us in motion, begins to work a transformation in the way we feel about ourselves and the way we act. Finding ourselves the object of a great love, we want to make our whole lives respond to it. We want to be more worthy of it, make some return on it, extend the range of its influence. The spiritual life of the Christian is always a response to an initiative taken by a God who first loves us.

This happened to Zaccheus suddenly and without warning, that day he climbed the sycamore tree to see Jesus (Lk. 19). He was a short man, and not much favored in the community because he was a tax collector and wealthy besides. A glimpse of Jesus was all he was asking, no interview. Unaccustomed as he was to being loved, his amazement can be imagined when Jesus stopped at the base of his tree, called him

by name, and asked him to hurry down because he wanted to
have lunch with him that day. So what does Zaccheus do?

> Zaccheus stood and said to the Lord, "Behold, Lord, the
> half of my goods I give to the poor; and if I have de-
> frauded anyone of anything, I restore it fourfold" (Lk.
> 19:8).

It reminds one of the contest between the North Wind and the
Sun to see which one could sooner get a traveler on the road
below to take off his coat. Needless to say, the warmth of the
Sun proved more powerful than the strength of the Wind. And
in the same way Jesus, with a little love, accomplishes in
Zaccheus what a hostile town, all in concert, never could. It is
yet another instance of G.K. Chesterton's paradoxical truth:
"A thing must be loved *before* it is lovable."

If we apply such an understanding of grace to our discussion of marriage, it seems safe to say that one's spouse is an
important channel of grace, perhaps even *the* most important
channel of grace in one's life. This may seem a bold claim,
especially to a theology which understands grace as this special sort of supernatural treasure flowing from certain religious
activities, notably prayer and the sacraments. But if grace is
most radically the graciousness of God turned toward us, then
does it not seem clear that our husband or wife, as the key
figure in our lives where love and closeness are concerned, will
be a main channel, perhaps the main channel, of this gentle
influence of God? Not that prayer and sacraments lose their
validity as such channels; they have their own way of speaking
and mediating God's graciousness. They celebrate, and height-
en our awareness of, the grace of God meeting us everywhere.
But what we need to appreciate more deeply is God's presence
and creative action as mediated to us by significant persons in
our everyday experience. And one's spouse is probably the
highest instance of this for married people.

The Paschal Mystery

We come finally to the theological notion which is at the heart of Christianity, that of the death and resurrection of Christ and their significance for us. We call it the paschal mystery. At a primary level, it is not so difficult to understand. Jesus died for our sins, the New Testament tells us, and God raised him from the dead. This is our salvation. It clearly reveals the love of God for us, and authenticates Jesus as witness in all that he said. The proper response is gratitude to God for all he has done for us, and an effort to conform our lives to the teaching and example of Jesus.

But many texts in the New Testament suggest that there are other dimensions of meaning to these events than their having taken place for us some 2000 years ago in testimony of God's love. These texts suggest that there is something contemporaneous about the death and resurrection of the Lord.

For while we live we are always being given up to death for Jesus' sake, so that the life of Jesus may be manifested in our mortal flesh. So death is at work in us, but life in you (2 Cor. 4:11-12).

. . . That I may know him and the power of his resurrection, and may share his sufferings, becoming like him in his death, that if possible I may attain the resurrection from the dead (Phil. 3:10-11).

But if Christ is in you, although your bodies are dead because of sin, your spirits are alive because of righteousness. If the Spirit of him who raised Jesus from the dead dwells in you, he who raised Jesus from the dead will give life to your mortal bodies also through his Spirit which dwells in you (Rom. 8:10-11).

What these passages indicate is that we today are somehow involved in the pattern of the death and resurrection of the Lord, that what happened to him happens also to us, and that it happens to us in him. In other words, in his experience is revealed to us the pattern by which all creation moves forward—dying and then rising again to new life. When the risen Jesus confronts the unbelief of his disciples, the saying with which he upbraids them is:

> O foolish men, and slow of heart to believe all that the prophets have spoken. Was it not necessary that the Christ should suffer these things and enter into his glory?" And beginning with Moses and all the prophets, he interpreted to them in all the Scriptures the things concerning himself (Lk. 24:25-27).

So too in the upper room:

> Then he opened their minds to understand the Scriptures, and said to them, "Thus it is written that the Christ should suffer and on the third day rise from the dead" (Lk. 24:45-46).

Jesus is referring in a summary way to the entire Old Testament, presenting the heart of its message in precisely the terms of his own passover experience, death and resurrection. And when he says that this pattern is already at least adumbrated in the Old Testament revelation, he is saying that it can be seen at work in the lives of all the generations which have gone before, and so has come into the awareness of the prophets, the psalmists, and the historians: life moves forward not continuously and triumphantly from expansion to expansion, but rather through a strange process of death and new birth. The pattern is most resplendently manifest in the death of Jesus and his resurrection to new and fuller life. But it is already dimly discernible in nature, as the darkness of night gives way to the light of dawn, as the storm yields to calm, as winter warms to spring, as the caterpillar turns into the butterfly, as the withering flower scatters new seed or the mature animal

29

generates its own kind before it dies. Jesus' favorite metaphor for the mystery is the seed:

> Truly, truly I say to you, unless a grain of wheat falls into the earth and dies, it remains alone; but if it dies, it bears much fruit (Jn. 12:24).

And when he applies it to human life, his expression is:

> Whoever would save his life will lose it; and whoever loses his life for my sake will save it (Lk. 9:24).

We experience this paradoxical law of growth all through our lives, and in all circumstances. But here we are interested chiefly in its typical embodiments in marriage. The whole theme of Gail Sheehy's bestseller, *Passages*, is that there are difficult times in life through which we must painfully pass that we might become more fully ourselves. A human relationship knows many such passages. It too has critical periods when some kind of death is taking place and is heavily felt; and it too knows resurrection from the dead. Married people experience occasions when communication is very difficult, almost too forbidding even to attempt. Yet it is a matter of testimony that if the difficulty is faced and the risk taken, out of that dying comes new life in the relationship. Marriages run into days when all seems lost and nothing could bring recovery; yet recovery somehow miraculously occurs, and what seemed dead comes to life again. Married people know stages when a whole previous mode of relating is no longer suitable, no longer works, and it has to be laid aside with no certitude as to what might be born to take its place. Yet something is born, and then the two can look back and see that the new is better than the old. All living is leave-taking, and the subsequent greeting of the unfamiliar. So it is in loss of job or of health, in changing interests, in forced farewell to certain earlier supports. So it is in the coming and again in the going of children, in the diminishment of physical beauty and vigor, in the loss of faculties and powers. If a marriage is growing, it is growing through deaths and resurrections. If it is not growing, it might be because there is a refusal to die the deaths that have to be died and to seek in them the direction in which new life is breaking. If Jesus, for fear, had refused to die, he would not know the kind of life he now knows as risen Lord, nor would we have the gift of his Spirit.

A Christian is a person whose great privilege it is to know the secret of the Kingdom of God. That secret is the paschal mystery, the code-key for understanding all that happens in this world. Just as we cannot attain to the life which is our final fulfillment without passing through the dark and usually painful death of our bodies, so, more generally, we cannot attain to the deeper and fuller dimensions of human existence without passages of a similar kind. Death is no fun, but resurrection is, and when it is attained we are happy we died the death. Some deaths are undergone quickly. In other dimensions of our being, the dying process seems to go on most of our years. Such is the death to selfishness, for example, or to fear, to anxiety, or to some of our other slaveries. But whether it be a quick death or a slow one, a superficial death or a radical one, our entire human experience is subsumed into the death and resurrection of Christ, for we are his Body. And so a Christian is not surprised when death knocks and darkness visits the heart, nor does a Christian lose hope. Insofar as possible we try to surrender ourselves to those deaths in the spirit of Jesus, who gave himself over freely and in trust. He did it, and we do it, because we have learned to believe in God "who gives life to the dead and calls into existence the things that do not exist" (Rom. 4:17). We stake our hopes on

> ... the immeasurable greatness of his power in us who
> believe, according to the working of his great might which

31

he accomplished in Christ when he raised him from the dead and made him sit at his right hand in the heavenly places (Eph. 1:19-20).

A very important part of the theology of marriage is to realize that both the individuals involved, and the relationship itself, are caught up in the mystery of the death and resurrection of Christ.

Suggestions for Further Reading

Karl Rahner, *Revelation and Tradition*
Avery Dulles, *Revelation Theology*
Juan Luis Segundo, *Grace and the Human Condition*
Gregory Baum, *Man Becoming*

Chapter Four
LOVE ONE ANOTHER

The Church is the sacrament of Christ. And we have seen that that means Christians are the sacrament of Christ. Now the Christian home is certainly one of the primary embodiments of the Church, a microcosmic Christian society. We can rightly expect God to be there, for "Where two or three are gathered in my name, there am I in the midst of them" (Mt. 18:20). And in any such part of the Body of Christ, we can rightly expect revelation and grace and the paschal mystery to be at work. In this chapter, we shall explore these things in more detail, taking our cue from the principal New Testament text on marriage, the fifth chapter of the Letter to the Ephesians.

Way of Life as Sacrament

Marriage is a sacrament. This is often understood to mean that the ritual action in which two people commit themselves to one another before God is a sacrament, and theological reflection has tended to center around that moment. Yet it would seem far more fruitful to look upon that moment as the initiation of a whole sacramental state, and to examine the state as the main sacramental reality. For the

33

meaning of that momentary transaction only comes clear, and can only come clear, as the life which it begins unfolds in all its dimensions. In this there are parallels with the sacraments of baptism and orders, to name only two. For in these cases also, the reality of the sacrament is only clearly seen in the subsequent state, a human life which has a certain kind of sacramentality or transparency to the divine. From the point of view of grace too, we have seen the inadequacy of speaking of the grace of the sacrament of matrimony, or of the other sacraments, as if it were some supernatural quantity all given in the ritual of a moment. Grace is rather the graciousness of God surrounding our lives at all times, reaching us through many channels, adapted to our personal and communal circumstances. Ritual sacraments highlight this fact, remind us of it, celebrate it, and thereby intensify it. So our consideration of matrimony as a sacrament is a consideration not primarily of a ritual action, but of a whole state of life which can truly be called sacramental.

We come now to the key New Testament text on marriage. It contains most of the important elements of a Christian theology of marriage, and so we quote it at length, with just one prenote. The sexism of the passage should be for the moment indulged. More on this shortly.

> Be subject to one another out of reverence for Christ. Wives, be subject to your husbands, as to the Lord. For the husband is the head of the wife as Christ is the head of the Church, his body, and is himself its savior. As the Church is subject to Christ, so let wives also be subject in everything to their husbands. Husbands, love your wives, as Christ loved the Church and gave himself up for her, that he might sanctify her, having cleansed her by the washing of water with the word, that he might present the Church to himself in splendor, without spot or wrinkle or any such thing, that she might be holy and without blemish. Even so husbands should love their wives as their own

bodies. He who loves his wife loves himself. For no man ever hates his own flesh, but nourishes and cherishes it, as Christ does the Church, because we are members of his body. "For this reason a man shall leave his father and mother and be joined to his wife, and the two shall become one flesh." This mystery is a profound one, and I am saying that it refers to Christ and the Church; however let each one of you love his wife as himself, and let the wife see that she respects her husband (Eph. 5:21-33).

This text needs to be rehabilitated a bit to be acceptable in the present age. It is sexist. No writer rises completely above his or her own time, and that includes the biblical writers. The culture of the New Testament was male-dominated, and New Testament writings simply take this for granted as they take slavery and a three-storied cosmos for granted. Now there is male-domination in our own day too, but we at least begin to know better and are taking steps to remedy the situation. Looking at the text above from today's perspective, there is really no more reason for wives to be subject to their husbands than for husbands to be subject to their wives. Nor is it any truer that husbands lay down their lives for their wives than that wives lay down their lives for their husbands. These relationships are fully mutual and can be so understood without taking anything away from the text. Another reason why it is written as it is is that in the parallel with Christ and the Church, he, of course, is masculine and the Church is thought of as feminine in relation to him. But no parallel is perfect. It is clear that a wife can be Christ to her husband (or anyone else) in the sense of the text, just as well as he can be Christ to her.

These things having been said, the main idea in the passage is that marriage images something about the way Christ is related to the Church. This is what we have referred to as the sacramentality of married life, its capacity as sign to make visible something otherwise invisible, as part of the sacramentality of the whole Church. Again it must be remembered that Church means people, Christians, So what we are talking about is the way Christ loves people, and the thesis is that Christian marriage reveals that kind of love, or should. Now that is quite a vocation.

Christ and the Church

How does Christ love people? The answer is in the Gospels. He loves them as they are. He meets them where they are, with open acceptance. Magdalen is a repentant sinner, and he gives her welcome (Lk. 7). Zaccheus is apparently shy, a social outcast, and a man with a questionable financial record. Jesus reaches out to him (Lk. 19). Peter is impetuous, good-hearted but blundering, and he doesn't know himself very well. The Lord bears with him, schools him, forgives him, makes him head of the Church (Mt. 16, Jn. 21). The Twelve generally are, like most of us, a little dense, and too often in pursuit of the wrong goals. The Lord remains faithful to them, both challenges and patiently instructs them, gives them responsibility. A widow comes out of a village in the funeral procession of her only real joy, a son, and Jesus restores him to her (Lk. 7). A wealthy young man shows interest in going beyond the minimum in his service of God, and Jesus challenges him to the fullest generosity (Mk. 10). Children approach him, and he takes them on his lap (Mk. 10). A woman is caught in adultery and made a public spectacle, and he rescues her from the crowd, saves her from capital punishment, and tells her she is forgiven (Jn. 8). A blind man diffidently calls from the side of the road, and Jesus halts his entire entourage, calls the man over, and restores his sight (Mk. 10). Wherever he encounters hypocrisy, he confronts it. Where he finds disease, he heals it. Where he sees unfreedom, whether it stems from law, from guilt, or from inner compulsion, he liberates. Paul summarizes Jesus' whole ministry in the words: "God was in Christ, reconciling the world to

36

himself, not counting people's offenses against them" (2 Cor. 5:19). For Jesus was surely the incarnation of the faithful, merciful love of God. And his revelation of God comes to its fullest clarity in his self-sacrifice for us on the cross, his passage to new life, and his gift to the Church of his Spirit.

Now it must always be borne in mind for whom he does these things. It is for sinners, i.e., humankind. Not for a few good folks, but for all of us. Not for an ideal world, but for the real world, broken, selfish, hard-hearted, inconstant, saying one thing and doing another, grasping, violent, ungrateful, suffering, guilty, and sad, pitiful, scarcely understanding itself and not sure what to do. This is the real human race for which Christ died, and to which he continues to give himself.

Love One Another

"Husbands and wives, love one another as Christ loved the Church and gave himself up for her" (Eph. 5:25). Now we can better understand what that injunction means, what kind of love it is that Christian marriage is intended to incarnate. It is self-giving love, and its object is the unworthy sinner. It is creative love, bringing the other to wholeness and holiness. It is faithful love, abiding and there to be relied upon even when all rightful claim has been forfeited. This is a weighty charge, yet our text unmistakably brings marriage right into line with Christ's way of loving his Church.

> "For this reason a man shall leave his father and mother and be joined to his wife, and the two shall become one flesh." This mystery is a profound one, and I am saying that it refers to Christ and the Church (Eph. 5:31-32).

The sacramentality of Christian marriage has a double aspect. It is, like the Church itself, partly revelation to those outside, partly revelation to those within. The Christian family, like the Church itself, is "a city set on a hill" for all around it to see, that God might be glorified (Mt. 5:14-16). But this revelation has an internal aspect too. Husbands and wives themselves (and their children, for that matter) need to be able to perceive Christ's love coming to them in the other. It answers a deep human need, a profound lurking doubt. How many of us really believe in God's love for ourselves? We may assent to the abstract proposition that he loves the whole world. We may even say in a notional way that he loves us. But do we really believe it in our hearts, with sufficient conviction to rely on it? How can this invisible love be brought home to us? It needs to touch us unmistakably at the level of human incarnation or sacramentality.

That is why the experience of falling in love has such tremendous power. For many people, it is the first time in their lives that they have felt deeply loved. Me? Loved by this person in a special way? Why? How amazing! How wonderful! From this experience half the poetry of the world and half the songs are written. For the people who change our lives the most, even where faith is concerned, are not usually the preachers, but those few simple folks who genuinely love us. They put flesh on the truth, and then it touches not just our minds but our very selves. This is the power of incarnation. "No one has ever seen God. The only-begotten Son, who is in the bosom of the Father, has made him known" (Jn. 1:18). And just as Jesus, in the flesh, makes the love of God tangible and effective, so anyone who loves us makes the whole intangible truth of God's love for us sinners a fact of experience.

Most husbands and most wives need that incarnate experience, to move their belief in the love of God from a merely notional level to the bedrock of conviction. By the time we reach adulthood, we have usually had enough experiences of total or at least partial rejection, and enough insight into our own complex and not altogether beautiful selves that we really need healing, the kind of healing that only a devoted and total

38

kind of loving can bring. And we need it not just once, but again and again, because our doubts persist. Now married love is not just the love of a moment, but the love of a lifetime. It is not a naive love, but a mature love that has come to see weakness and fault and goes on anyway. Its fidelity and its fullness are the most complete incarnation of God's kind of love for the flawed and fragile human persons that we are. And what it incarnates it also mediates, so that it is God's own love, not just an imitation of it, that is received. He loves us through one another.

Whether we speak in purely human terms or in the language of faith, there is no greater gift anyone can give anyone than the simple act of loving him or her. It makes all the difference. Without that experience, our whole lives flounder about, and we are caught in a hundred unfreedoms. That experience in place, we breathe deeply, smile, laugh, love, and bring energy and enthusiasm to life. We are redeemed.

If we are going to love in Christ, we have to learn from him how to do it. We have seen the scope and generosity of his love. Let us look for a moment at its technique. As we study the Gospels, or consult our own spiritual history, we notice that his loving carefully combines challenge and comfort. Almost any passage chosen from the Gospels will be an instance of the one or the other. Either he is challenging us, pushing us on from the place we are, calling our understanding or practice into question and indicating a better alternative, exposing our hypocrisy or half-heartedness, setting a higher ideal before us. Or he is comforting us, assuring us that we are accepted in spite of our sinfulness, telling us that in our pain a mysterious process is at work which leads toward something richer. Challenge and comfort, the two in alternation, is the model he works from, and the combination is fruitful not only in adult relationships, but in the way parents must love and raise their children. Too much challenge leaves the person loved feeling unloved, never good enough, never measuring up, always in the wrong. Too much comfort breeds self-satisfaction and stasis at low levels of development. Jesus uses now the one, now the other, in deft combination. So must we. Sometimes a husband or wife needs nothing so much as unconditional acceptance. Some days the world batters one pretty badly. Often the world demands that we wear masks. Sometimes our own inner demons give us a particularly tough go of it. These are the times we need comfort, some one human being who knows our whole story and can embrace it with a large heart. Other times, we need to hear a painful truth spoken to us with love, need to be brought to face ourselves. We need to be made to accept responsibility for what we have said or done, or to be pressed to make the move we know we should make but don't want to. These are the times the best way to love us is to challenge us.

There are other important qualities in Christ's love too. He is patient. He never violates a person's freedom, never forces anything, always only invites and waits. He loves the truth, and always speaks the truth in love. He is solicitous to serve, and seeks ways to express himself in service. His love is always quietly present, rescuing from difficulty, freeing from bondage, surprising with unexpected gifts. It is gentle. It is compassionate and merciful. It is above all things faithful, in good times and in bad, true to its covenant. It is self-sacrificing, not surprised at the cost, not eager to find an exit.

Ephesians tells us Christ loves the Church as his own body. He loves us from within, and with the instinctiveness with which anyone loves and cares for his or her very self. And so it is in marriage, where two become one flesh, not just physically but in the total sense in which two whole lives in all their dimensions are intertwined. That is the married ideal. The poet, e.e. cummings, captures the spirit of it when he says:

> i carry your heart with me (i carry it in
> my heart) i am never without it (anywhere

i go you go,my dear;and whatever is done
by only me is your doing,my darling)

                                             i fear
no fate (for you are my fate,my sweet) i want
no world (for beautiful you are my world,my true)

It should now be evident what a sublime and difficult vocation Christian marriage is, and what an important role it plays in the life of the Church. It should also be clear how greatly the dimension of faith enriches this form of life which human nature so naturally seeks. Revelation, grace, sacramentality, the paschal mystery are all involved. For marriage springs from Christ, and is rooted and grounded in him. What he says about himself as good shepherd summarizes most of what we have seen here, again posing the ideal for married couples in their love for one another and for their children.

I am the good shepherd. The good shepherd lays down his life for the sheep. He who is a hireling and not a shepherd, whose own the sheep are not, sees the wolf coming and leaves the sheep and flees; and the wolf snatches them and scatters them. He flees because he is a hireling and cares nothing for the sheep. I am the good shepherd; I know my own and my own know me, as the Father knows me and I know the Father; and I lay down my life for the sheep (Jn. 10:11-15).

Chapter Five

SEX

One of the most interesting things in the whole world is sex. It is also a constant puzzlement. So maybe not a few people will read this chapter first. It is not the most important chapter in the book, but if a book on marriage is wrong on sex, the flaw is serious. If it is right on sex, people who have much less interest in theology may take a chance on some of the other chapters. This is not an unfair test. Sex is important, and a good reality-indicator. The criterion by which any treatment of it is legitimately tested is the criterion of experience. Either the theory will correspond with experience or it will not. Unfortunately, much of what is said about sex from a theological point of view does not correspond with experience, and then people are forced to a difficult choice: either to write off the theology, or to deny their own experience in face of the authority of theology. Neither is desirable. Why can't the two correspond? We need a good theology of sex. The present chapter will attempt something along these lines for sex in marriage. But that is also the limit of our undertaking. We do not attempt a general sexual ethic and treat such issues as masturbation, homosexuality, or extramarital sex. We treat sex only in the context of marriage and explore its Christian meaning there.

The extraordinary power sex has over us seems to go beyond rational accounting. Its lure is larger than any possible presentation of the phenomenon. We think about it often, dream about it, joke about it. Our language is filled with sexual allusions, and they are seldom missed even when they are not intended, so close is sex to habitual awareness. Our interest in other persons often has a sexual dimension, and not infrequently a prominent one. Nothing makes quite such sensational news as sex scandals, and few magazines sell as well as the better pornography numbers. Pornography lives on public demand, and the demand has made it a huge industry. We do things sexually which, in more reflective moments, puzzle us and leave us sometimes remorseful. In short, we are fascinated with sex, and it has great power over us. Freud thought that all human motivation was rooted sexually. Psychology since Freud generally regards that as an exaggeration, but like most exaggerations, it houses a truth.

It might seem bold to suggest that our fascination with sex is closely related to our fascination with God, but the possibility suggests itself. Some may not recognize that they have a fascination with God; they don't think about him much. But our fascination with God is the restlessness of our hearts, and that, in some measure or other, is always with us. George Herbert's poem "The Pulley" names "rest" as the one gift God did not give us, lest we repose in his gifts and forget about him; and St. Augustine's best known one-liner is probably: "Thou hast made us for thyself, O Lord, and our hearts are restless until they rest in thee." It touches a chord. If all human living is marked by that nameless thirst for a mystery we call God, and if sex, with its lure, powerfully claims a quantity of that energy to itself, can they be unrelated? Is sex simply false quest, a poor substitute for what we really want?

Or is it more likely one of the more compelling presentations of the mystery we call God, one of the more telling creative words in which he speaks his own self? The latter hypothesis seems the better commended. And in that case, sex and God are not in competition, like light and darkness.

"God is love," John's first letter tells us (1 Jn. 4:8). And there is a profound clue in that. For whether it be the nervous young fellow who stands waiting on the street corner for a pickup, the older man who pays his money and walks into a porno theater, the woman in her thirties who straightens her hair and heads for the cocktail lounge on a Saturday night, or the fellow from the gas station who keeps asking for a date, love is the common quest. Sex does not always give love, of course, but surely that is its great promise and the thing most deeply sought—closeness, intimacy, tenderness, joy. The fact that we are sexual beings, male or female, is the sign of our incompleteness. And the physical has a correlative in the realm of spirit, that profound feeling of emptiness, of need for some other, the thirst for completion by someone. Again e.e. cummings says it well:

> i am a birdcage without any bird,
> a collar looking for a dog, a kiss without lips

It is the same human need that drives us toward sex (with love) and God for our completion. And though sex is obviously not God, and our restlessness will continue no matter how good our circumstances as long as we are in this world, a good case can be made for the idea that God, being love and self-revealing, might be speaking to us through his creation of sex in a uniquely eloquent way.

Up from Guilt

If we look back at what we have heard about sex from a religious standpoint, there would probably be few who could show any but negative recollections. The Christian churches of our acquaintance have presented sex as mostly a dangerous thing, if not a positively bad thing. It is something not to be thought upon, still less spoken of, and every precaution must be taken against the least lapse in deed. All this is very familiar, and accounts for the fact that any sexual deviation from the proposed ideal incites feelings of guilt and shame which are deep and lasting. Marriage, of course, is a different case. Sex there is all right. Once you cross that threshold you can do it. It is a concession God grants to help people bear the burdens of married responsibility. Even here there are things to be guarded against, of course, but in marriage most sex is allowed. Such is the classical presentation. Christian theological concern has concentrated so much on moral questions about sexuality, with typically defensive and negative stands, that sex has come to be the moral issue of greatest concern in the popular mind. If people have no sexual wrong on their consciences, they think they have no sin, at least nothing of any consequence. This is a serious distortion of the New Testament.

Nothing could be more plain from a reading of the Gospels than that Jesus is simply not busy with sex. He has very little to say about it. He does not mention masturbation once. He says nothing about homosexuality. One looks in vain for some usable material on "impure thoughts," or a strong speech on the evils of fornication. About all there is to be found is a statement of the marital ideal of indissolubility, and a lot on love in general which has implications for the use of sex. There is nothing on birth control either. For every one time that Jesus says anything about sex, he speaks a hundred times about loving one's neighbor, trusting in God, being grateful for life and all its gifts, forgiving injuries, not accumulating riches but sharing all things, bearing sufferings patiently and in hope, helping the person in need, not being anxious, being prayerful. And whenever anyone comes up who has done something wrong sexually, Jesus promptly forgives. These things we have seen. Now given his manifest attitude toward the body, sex, love, marriage, all that pertains to ordinary human life, and the almost complete lack of anything in the Gospels which is condemning or even strongly cautionary where sex is concerned, is it not remarkable that the Church, his Body, has made sex *the* moral issue for the Christian?

The moralists do have a legitimate concern. We are flawed, and there is disorder to be reckoned with in our sexual drives. Sex in human life is difficult to use well, to humanize fully, to integrate responsibly into mature personhood so that it becomes expressive as it ought to be of genuine love. But should this surprise us? Love is the most difficult thing of all, the supreme human achievement. It will take us all our lives to learn to love well all those various people with whom we have to deal, and the learning will come only through trial and error and the pains of growth. So it is with sex. Sexual integration and humanization too will take a lifetime and be accomplished only through trial and error and the pains of growth. Surely the Lord knows that and is at peace with it. It is he who sets us down not complete but self-creating. A little of that realization and accompanying peace would not hurt us either.

A Touch of His Glory

What can be said theologically of sex in marriage, if it be not negative moral guidance? It could probably be said that married people should expect some of the more important religious experiences of their lives in bed. That may sound blasphemous to some ears. It is not what we usually hear in church. But does that not show how far we have separated religion and life? Isn't it God who has designed this whole thing we call sex, giving us the capacity, the desire, and the fulfillment? The idea is his, and surely it is a great gift to us. Our unspoiled response is gratitude, wonder, and celebration, not just for a human endowment created long ago, but for his gift of the same to me this day. Most married people would probably name the sexual expression of their love one of their greatest joys. Can we make no connection between this and our belief in God's love for us? Could he say it better? In the hearts of those to whom good sexual experience is given, it will surely be an important item when they say at worship: "Blessed are you, Lord, God of all creation!"

But there is more. He is in the gift he gives, and that is why we can say that sex will mediate the experience of God. Married love is sacramental; it makes the invisible visible and tangible. But where is married love more tellingly told than in its sexual expression? Then isn't this too the word of God incarnate?

> Beloved, let us love one another; for love is of God, and
> the person who loves is born of God and knows God.
> Anyone who does not love does not know God, for God is
> love (1 Jn.4:7-8).

> So we know and believe the love God has for us. God is
> love, and the person who abides in love abides in God and
> God in that person (1 Jn. 4:16).

If God is love, he must be present where human love is most powerfully spoken. Where will we better encounter his closeness, his gentleness, his tenderness? His acceptance of us as we are? His fidelity? Is not physical tenderness in the expression of devoted love the bearer of his healing, to the depths of ourselves, in the only way that healing or anything else can reach our human spirits—somehow through the medium of our bodies? Surely in sex we have a revelation of God the lifegiver, refreshing and renewing us, making us peaceful and happy, deepening the meaning of our lives, kindling again our

48

own capacity to love. And do we not have in the experience of unity between two persons, both physically and in the deeper communication of spirit which sexual union facilitates, a taste of the union that obtains between Christ and his Father in the Spirit, and between Christ and ourselves?

> The glory which you have given me I have given to them, that they may be one even as we are one, I in them and you in me, that they may become perfectly one, so that the world may know that you have sent me and have loved them even as you have loved me (Jn. 17:22-23).

Our God is a God of play too, not of seriousness only. Look at the children he makes, and how beautiful and expressive they are at play. Look at the animals, the ostrich and the rhinoceros, the chipmunk, the otter, and the porpoise and the seal, fishes' faces and hopping birds. Much of God's world is at play, and calls us to play. Sex is play, and the child in us loves it. It has inspired much humor and plenty of laughter, and well it might. In sex we know God's light side, as well as his tender. Sex is the celebration of life, and God surely delights in our joys, as any father would who sees his children enjoying the gifts he has given.

The Body

Christianity is not a religion for angels, because human beings are not angels but incarnate spirits. We live in the world, and are in vital contact with it at all times or we perish. Central to Christianity is the incarnation of the Son of God, and his media are material. It is in the Eucharist that we best and most frequently remember him and recognize his presence, and the Eucharist is based entirely on two profoundly human realities—the hosting of a meal, and the gift of the body. Jesus did not just convene a meal, which is already a

49

very communicative symbol. He also gave the gift of his body. We know the meaning of the gift of the body, whether it be the mother breast-feeding her infant, the adult sheltering or comforting the child, or, perhaps most expressively of all, husband and wife giving the gift of their bodies to one another. It is the gift of the self. Whenever that is done, there is an echo of Jesus' words, "This is my Body, for you." Marriage illuminates the meaning of the Eucharist. The Eucharist illuminates the meaning of marriage.

"Do you not know that your body is a temple of the Holy Spirit within you, which you have from God?" St. Paul asks (1 Cor. 6:19). Or, in a similar vein, "Like living stones be yourselves built into a spiritual house, to be a holy priesthood, to offer spiritual sacrifices acceptable to God through Jesus Christ" (1 Pet. 2:4-5). In these and other ways the New Testament states the truth that the whole idea of the Temple has shifted, from a building to human beings. The place of God's presence, first the Ark of the Covenant which the Hebrews transported from place to place in their wanderings, then the great sacred building in Jerusalem after they had settled in the Promised Land, shifts to the Body of Jesus, and thence to the Church, his complete body. This is the meaning of that saying:

"Destroy this temple, and in three days I will raise it up."
. . . But he spoke of the temple of his body (Jn. 2:19-21).

Because this represented so radical a shift in religious thinking, Jesus' contemporaries had a great deal of difficulty accepting it, and made it a major accusation against him at his trial (Mt. 26:61). A similar statement by Stephen became one of the principal causes of his martyrdom (Acts 7:13-14). The statement is revolutionary because it means that God is to be found not so much on a sacred mountain, or in a sacred building, but in the persons of human beings; that it is not the sacred vessel, the temple, or the church, but the ordinary person who most deserves our reverence. Thus the place of the significant religious encounter is moved back to the midst of life.

If contemporary theology has a dominant theme, it is this recovery of the sacred within the supposedly secular, the overcoming of the false dichotomy between natural and supernatural, the finding of God in the midst of ordinary life. Teilhard's cosmic Christ, Karl Rahner's horizon of mystery, Paul Tillich's ground of being, Peter Berger's signals of transcendence—all point to the same basic truth: God is in our midst. And the human person is a privileged bearer of the ultimate mystery. That is why Jesus says, "As you did it to one of the least of these my brothers or sisters, you did it to me" (Mt. 25:40). Or why he puts the question to Saul, persecutor of Christians: "Saul, Saul, why do you persecute me?" (Acts 9:4). His emphasis is spoken clearly also in the injunction:

> So if you are offering your gift at the altar, and there remember that your brother or sister has something against you, leave your gift there before the altar and go; first be reconciled to your brother or sister, and then come and offer your gift (Mt. 5:23-24).

We cannot suddenly turn toward the Lord at the altar when we turn away from him in human beings. This of course has tremendous implications for the whole of Christian spirituality. But the particular application of interest in the present context is that the body of one's spouse is the temple of the Lord. And the sexual encounter might well be one of those times in which one feels most prompted to say in one's heart, adapting the psalmist: "How lovely is your dwelling place, O Lord of hosts" (Ps. 84).

Integration is what we deeply want, the capacity to embrace the various elements of reality whole. Christianity, an incarnate and sacramental religion, goes further than any of the major religions in offering possibilities for the synthesis of matter and spirit. It is one of the happy developments of our time that the Christian experience of bodiliness and sex, long tainted by Platonic dichotomies, presses the demand again for the articulation of an integrated spirituality.

Suggestions for Further Reading

A. Kosnick *et al., Human Sexuality*
Joseph and Lois Bird, *The Freedom of Sexual Love*
Evelyn Duvall, *Why Wait till Marriage?*
Walter Trobisch, *I Loved a Girl*
Teilhard de Chardin, *The Divine Milieu*
Paul Tillich, *The Dynamics of Faith*
Peter Berger, *A Rumor of Angels*

Chapter Six
CHILDREN

"Children are a gift of God," the psalmist says (Ps. 127), and so it seems at times. More than one set of parents has testified that bringing their first child into the world was the greatest religious experience of their lives. They were awestruck, in the religious sense, when they beheld the emergence of the tiny new human being, their own co-creation, and received it as a gift of God. They saw in the infant a concrete embodiment of their love for one another, and a great new responsibility. Now they knew the meaning of the words:

> When a woman is in labor, she has sorrow because her hour has come; but when she has brought forth, she no longer remembers the anguish for joy that a child is born into the world (Jn. 16:21).

Children do us a great favor. They bring us back to life. They invite us to rediscover the world. The basic stance of the child toward the world is one of wide-eyed wonder. They stand and stare, taking it all in in amazement; then they want to touch it, whatever it is, and if possible put it in their mouths. As they grow, their horizons broaden, and they keep calling us out to see and to do things we've stopped seeing and forgotten how to do. The zoo is for them, and the park; campgrounds and Disneyland. Mothers play house again, and fathers limber up to play baseball. It is a delight to discover San Francisco or New York for the first time, and a delight again to show them to someone else. And so it is with the world. It's fun to show children around and watch their reactions. Many a modern theologian finds the cause of people's difficulty in knowing God today in their loss of wonder at the world. We have become technologists and managers, and no longer really see the materials we manipulate. If anyone can reawaken the sense of wonder that leads to the contemplation of God, it is the children of this world. They are a gift of freshness.

In fact, they are themselves a revelation of God. His beauty is resplendent in their faces, voices, movements, and in the fresh spontaneity of their reactions and replies. The poet, Gerard Manley Hopkins, captures it when he says:

> For Christ plays in ten thousand places, lovely in limbs,
> and lovely in eyes not his, to the Father, in the features of
> men's faces.

Children speak profound truths with an effortlessness that makes the adult despair at times. They play in the world with reckless abandon, and disarm the crustiest of us with their implicit trust. They teach us many things. Jesus says:

> "Let the children come to me, do not hinder them; for to
> such belongs the kingdom of God. Truly, I say to you,
> whoever does not receive the kingdom of God like a child
> shall not enter it." And he took them in his arms and
> blessed them, laying his hands upon them (Mk. 10:14-16).

The Cost of Creation

"Children are a gift of God," the psalmist says, and so it seems at times. At other times not. What the psalmist does not note, at least in this psalm, is that the bearing and raising of children take just about everything we've got. Theologically, this project is most closely allied to God's work of creation.

Time was, not so long ago, when God's work of creation was considered as something accomplished once and for all. Even where it was not thought of as achieved in an instant by a divine act of the will bringing all things out of nothingness, it was conceived of as taking place within a relatively brief span of time, a week of "days," "in the beginning," (Gen. 1). And once creation had taken place, God's relationship to the world was thought of as conservation and providence.

A more evolutionary perspective on cosmic history has changed that notion of creation significantly. Needless to say, the biblical writers did not have such an evolutionary perspective. But that is not so terribly significant, since their purpose was not to tell how things had come to be, but to state that the world *is* creation, i.e., that it is a derivative, dependent reality, with its source in God. This they expressed imaginatively, in terms and concepts that came naturally to them in their world of thought. We are entitled to do the same, understanding the identical basic truth in ways compatible with our own world of thought. And prominent in our world of thought is the realization of evolution. From what we now know of cosmic history, God created not so much a world as the raw materials for a world. What we find in the early stages are simple elements, and what we see over time is those simple elements being organized into more complex entities in a process that goes on and on and is still far from complete. On this understanding of things, it becomes very difficult to draw the line between where creation ends and conservation and providence begin. In fact, it is impossible, and it makes more sense from many points of view to say that God is always creating. But he does not do this in direct and dramatic ways, dropping fully formed entities from the sky, but in mediated and ordinary ways, creating through us and other this-worldly agencies. He creates as we create.

And so it is with the children of the human family. In this work, parents are co-creators with God from beginning to end. Earlier theology had made this point with respect to the conception of life in the womb. But a more complete understanding demands that it be extended to the years-long work of fashioning genuine human persons. For in the case of children too, what conception and even birth deliver are not so much a human person as the raw materials of a human person. And fashioning those elements into a person will be a creative task of immense exertion. To this any parent can attest. God labors over his creation. Parents do too. It is the same labor, the one within the other. Paul tells us:

> We know that the whole creation has been groaning in travail until now. . . . For the creation waits with eager longing for the revealing of the sons and daughters of God (Rom. 8:19-23).

And he speaks of the people of Galatia as "my little children, with whom I am again in labor until Christ be formed in you" (Gal. 4:19).

The Master's Technique

And how is this creative work to be done? That is a hard question, and theology has no blueprint for it. But if we place it in the context of faith, we can at least see it as cooperation in God's own creative labor of love, and we can learn something helpful about his approach to it from Jesus. For Jesus' work in our midst can properly be viewed as creative labor, a work of shaping and reshaping, of evoking and educing the best person each of us can be. "My Father is working still, and I am working" (Jn. 5:17).

There are moments of stern command and unambiguous condemnation in Jesus' dealings with people. Yet his favorite method seems to combine comfort and challenge, as we have seen, and a profound respect for human freedom. And it entails his own suffering. He evokes and educes, calls and invites. He does not come so much to add something to people as to call out of them what they can be and deeply want to be. He does not give them orders so that they will be exactly what he wants them to be and do what he wants them to do, all of this as an imposition from without. He rather frees them from the inauthenticity in themselves so they can be their genuine selves, calls to the deepest goodness within them so that it can emerge, models a pattern of human living so attractive that they become like him because they want to. In dealing with us as his own creative project, he alternatively comforts and challenges us. Sometimes he shows us that he accepts and loves us just as we are, wherever we may be on the trajectory of our unfolding; and sometimes he offers us a painful insight into ourselves or holds out an ideal not yet realized, urging us beyond the place where we are. He never violates our freedom. He forces nothing. He will take No for an answer, and scrap one plan for another if we force him to it. And this entails suffering for him and new efforts. We see him on the cross, the perfect embodiment of the weakness and power of love confronting the world. He will use no other kind of power. "And I, when I be lifted up from the earth, will draw all people to myself " (Jn. 12:32).

There are cues here for parents. Those who only comfort and never challenge, who always say Yes and never No, who give whatever is asked for, will spoil their children. But by the same token, those who are always criticizing and pushing toward the not yet attained, who give the impression that they would love their children "if only," or will begin to love them "as soon as," will ruin their children too. They will crush their spirits and leave them deeply scarred in self-doubt and self-rejection.

Respecting freedom and allowing it scope is another delicate matter. Even if perfect compliance can be won from a child under fear of punishment or hope of reward in the years of greatest dependency, education has not taken place until values are internalized as one's own and are freely chosen in one's autonomy as an adult. Many is the child who is successfully contained under a strict regime, and who later erupts and throws over *everything* he or she was taught. Freedom was never given its exercise. There is the subtler problem too of trying to live one's life over again in one's child. Thus Julie is to have strong intellectual and artistic interests because her mother does—or because her mother never did but wishes she had. And Bill is destined to work into his father's business and make it greater still—or he is supposed to do something completely different because his father wishes he himself had made a different choice. The son is supposed to become a priest, or the daughter a socialite even at a very early age, to make their parents proud. This is forcing the mould, and is bound to result in resentments and some very painful readjustments later. It shows a frightening insensitivity to freedom and individuality.

If parents show sensitivity, on the other hand, they let themselves in for the suffering of God himself in dealing with the freedom of his creation. In loving one another, parents learn what it is for Christ to love his sinful Church. They will find the same thing in loving their children. Many are the parents who wring their hands today because it is so difficult for them to accept their older children's choices. It may be the person a son or daughter chooses to marry who meets parental disapproval, or the fact that they live with someone before marriage, or their dropping out of school, or their choice no longer to go to church, to get a divorce, to leave the priest-hood, or to enter a line of work their parents frown on. "What can we do?" the troubled parents ask. Very little, really, especially if the children are adults. What could the parents' parents have done with them in times now past? Not so very much. Yet one very important thing. They could have gone on loving them, and remained loyal to them in spite of the disagreement. Why sacrifice the relationship? It most likely will not change the decision anyway. Sometimes the choices children make today are just as difficult for them to make as for their parents to accept, yet they seem to the children the best option open to them. And one of their greatest fears in taking them is precisely that they will lose their parents' love, a loss painful to contemplate. The world is rapidly changing, and the generation gap grows larger with the passing of the decades. Parental perspectives reflect the limitations of their own time and place, and may have to yield to guesses which may be just as good in a changed world. In any case, an essential part of loving seems to be to remain solid with people in their important life choices.

Religious Education

Not too long ago, particularly in Roman Catholicism, we Christians had a very elaborate system of private religious schools. We still have a rather considerable system, but, mostly because of a financial squeeze, we have had to curtail that system and move into a more streamlined approach through programs like the Confraternity of Christian Doctrine (CCD). What used to be a total education environment is thus reduced to a part-time specialized situation. But it has always been apparent to teachers working within either system that the primary influence on the children they teach is not their own. It is the home. If the task is well attended to at home, class is smooth sailing. If not, there is not too much that can be accomplished, toil how one will. The primary religious educators of children are their parents, whether they realize it or not. Positively or negatively, they teach the things most determinative of their children's outlook on life and of their behavior. There is no way parents can delegate that task to someone else and be rid of it. The transference is apparent only.

This will surely be frightening to some parents, who, either for lack of an intellectual grasp of their faith, or for lack of any serious commitment to it, feel they cannot handle the religious formation of their children. The first problem is not so serious. One need not be a theologian to pass on the faith to another person, since faith is not a body of doctrines to assent to in the mind, but a way of life to be embraced. In the Orient, the religious teacher is the guru, who is a model rather than an instructor, and with whom a young person lives so as to imbibe his spirit and assimilate his outlook and ways. So it is with religious education in the home. Christianity as a faith-vision of reality and a set of values governing choice is passed on from one person to another in implicit as well as explicit, non-verbal as well as verbal ways. Precision of concept is not the telling factor. Of course, the better one understands one's faith, in its bases, interrelationships, elaboration, and implications, the better equipped one is to pass it on to another. One would hope that any serious Christian will continue throughout life to seek a deeper understanding and surer grasp of faith's content, for one's own and others' sakes. But this is secondary rather than primary. The real problem for people is often the more serious deficiency of lack of any real commitment to the Christian life. Now if this is absent, outside influences hired for the formative task are severely limited in what they can accomplish. In fact, it becomes quite a contradiction in the mind of the child that his or her parents insist on an education which they do not take seriously themselves.

If Christianity is really going to be taught in the home,

parents will have to give some thought to times and methods. What is needed is not so much formal classes or instruction time, but the ability to seize occasions to inculcate the sort of understanding and attitudes that are involved. Thus, sex education will typically be done in response to the sorts of questions children ask as circumstances arise. A Christian attitude toward truth-telling, against acquisitiveness, toward responsible stewardship of environmental resources, respect for life, desire for peace, a spirit of forgiveness, love for all types of persons, sensitivity toward human need, hospitality to the stranger—all of these are taught as incidents in school, the neighborhood, or work are recounted in family conversation, or situations of choice arise in the home. Prayer is taught at the family table, and on special occasions either of family trouble or of extraordinary gratitude and celebration. Ritual celebrations are created around birthdays, new birth, baptism, the coming to maturity, sickness and recovery, major anniversaries, death, and so forth. The meaning of Christian faith, hope, and love are communicated by the way they are lived by adults. As inquiry arises directed toward a more conceptual grasp of the faith which is being lived, a new sort of answer needs to be provided. This is the proper place for CCD courses, adult education, and reading, as the effort continues through life to keep our grasp of the Christian message commensurate with our rising educational level and the sophistication of experience.

The important thing is to realize that Christianity is first a way of life, not a body of doctrines, and that it is taught by being modeled much more than by being explained. It is not the theologians to whom the Kingdom of God is promised, but to those who hear the word of God and keep it (Mt. 7:21). And Christianity as a way of life, a vision of things, a set of values, a spirit, is passed on first and most tellingly in the early formative years of a person's life by the primary influences upon that life, the parents. The goal sought is the goal of all the parents' creative effort, that for which the whole creation groans in eager expectation, the revealing of the sons and daughters of God.

There is a final important, obvious, and sometimes overlooked truth in the area of what parents can do for their children. They can love one another. This gives the children security and creates a warm and peaceful environment for their own life and growth. It also models the goal of their coming to maturity. It sometimes happens in a marriage that a man and woman become parents only. They spend themselves with the greatest generosity on their children, but they have lost touch with one another. At worst, their relationship is filled with rancor and alienation. At first unconsciously, then consciously, the children are affected by this, even if they are well loved by each parent singly. There is a saying that one of the greatest things a father can do for his children is to love their mother. The correlative is also true, that one of the greatest things a mother can do for her children is to love their father.

Suggestions for Further Reading

James Ewens, *Pass It On*
Piet Schoonenberg, *God's World in the Making*
Sigrid Undset, *Kristin Lavransdatter*

Chapter Seven

OUTREACH

The Church is conceived either as existing for itself or as existing for the world. On the former view, it is something we can escape into from the world, a sort of haven. What we do in church is considered the really important thing—prayer, the sacraments, and other church activities. The rest of our activity is secular. What goes on in church does not touch the world very much at all, except insofar as it fosters a morality which we live out in relationships on the outside. The Church has its concerns, the world a different set of concerns. The latter will pass away. The apostolate of the Church consists mainly in the effort to persuade people to join it. Thus, Church and world exist side by side, and the Church is more important than the world.

On the other view, the Church exists for the world, and it is for the sake of service to the world that Jesus founded it. It is a community of people, already living within the world and with no intention of going anyplace else, who want to spend themselves for the world's needs, as Jesus did. They do not seek to go apart any more than he did; they want to be involved. They do pray and gather for liturgical celebration, to keep their own vision and purpose strong. But their abiding desire is to serve wherever there is temporal or spiritual human distress. They want to reconcile people to one another, as Jesus did, and bring about that type of human community which was his dream and the inspiration of his whole effort. The Kingdom of God, insofar as we can realize it in the world, is a human community in which justice is observed and love prevails, God is Father and men and women are brothers and sisters, the goods of life are shared and care is shown for the well-being of all, across all lines of age, sex, race, culture, religion, and so forth. "For he is our peace, who has made us both one, and has broken down the dividing wall of hostility" (Eph. 2:14). Those who labor for this kingdom do not ask the poor, sick, or lost what their religion is; they meet them where they are and try to give them what they need. They do not ask those who want to collaborate with them what their religion is; they accept their common purpose and good will, confident that they are somehow rooted in the same God, regardless of how this relationship is articulated.

It is this latter conception of the Church that Vatican II endorses as the proper one. Religious concerns cannot be separated from the needs and aspirations of the earthly city. It is for the world that the Church exists.

> The joys and the hopes, the griefs and the anxieties of the people of this age, especially those who are poor or in any way afflicted, these too are the joys and hopes, the griefs and anxieties of the followers of Christ. Indeed nothing genuinely human fails to raise an echo in their hearts. . . . Inspired by no earthly ambition, the Church seeks but a solitary goal: to carry forward the work of Christ himself under the lead of the befriending Spirit. And Christ entered this world to give witness to the truth, to rescue and not to sit in judgment, to serve and not to be served (*The Church in the Modern World*, #1, #3).

Vatican II is also quite clear in addressing the mission of the Church to the laity in an essential way. This is already unambiguous in the *Dogmatic Constitution on the Church* and the *Pastoral Constitution on the Church in the Modern World*. But there is special stress on it in a separate document, the unprecedented *Decree on the Apostolate of the Laity*. The emphasis here is this great because the mission of the Church depends so vitally on an apostolic laity.

> Wishing to intensify the apostolic activity of the People of God, this most holy synod earnestly addresses itself to the laity, whose proper and indispensable role in the mission of the Church it has already called to mind in other documents. The lay person's apostolate derives from his or her Christian vocation, and the Church can never be without it. . . . In fact, modern conditions demand that this apostolate be thoroughly broadened and intensified (*Apostolate of the Laity,* #1).

In the present chapter, we shall look briefly at some of the apostolic possibilities that beckon to married Christians today.

Hospitality

There are some homes into which one can walk and find refreshment. There is hospitality, warmth, and the joy of life. Not that there isn't the usual struggle, imperfections, and unsolved problems, too much to do and too little time to do it in. But there is an upswing, a climate of humor and good will, an attitude of hopefulness, warm pep, and, above all, the sharing of life such as it is and the celebration of human togetherness. Such a place is an oasis for outsiders to come to, a place of peace, a home in which one feels welcome and from which one emerges refreshed in mind and spirit and recharged for the challenges and opportunities of life. To offer this kind of welcome and hospitality to people is surely to do Christian ministry in the best New Testament sense.

One of Jesus' most radical ideas is his idea for a party. Perhaps it has never been tried, but the scene he sketches takes strong hold on the imagination.

> When you give a dinner or a banquet, do not invite your friends or your brothers or your kinspeople or rich neighbors, lest they also invite you in return, and you be repaid. But when you give a feast, invite the poor, the maimed, the lame, the blind, and you will be blessed, because they cannot repay you. You will be repaid at the resurrection of the just (Lk. 14:12-14).

Imagine such a party! It would be an unforgettable experience. People would probably have a good time. It would certainly bust some stereotypes, give an exhilarating sense of the variety and mystery of human life, and provide plenty of matter for reflection. But perhaps the potion is too strong, and we fear to drink it. We prefer safety and manageableness, and the ordinary run of people who think, feel, and live as we do, and who will probably invite us back for another round of the same. But surely part of the beauty of the character of Jesus was his bold outreach in hospitality to every sort of sinner and social outcast. He knew the method of a good party. He outraged proper folk, who protested the company he kept, but he probably had better times than they.

There is another form of family ministry too. Some women do it at the kitchen table, listening to neighbors who drop in to talk. It is a tremendous opportunity to do someone some good, informal and unpretentious yet full of promise. People need to be listened to, need to be affirmed, need to hear common sense truths uttered again into their situation. A lot of problems cannot be solved, but they can be shared, and that makes them a great deal more tolerable. This too is a form of hospitality.

As one surveys the contemporary married scene, one of the needs that stands out is that for community among married couples. There is no way that any couple or any family can make it alone. The challenges are too great, and the resources of a single family unit too few. The extended family of aunts, uncles, cousins, grandparents, and in-laws has largely broken down, and the nuclear family itself faces strong forces of dissolution. Its members need encouragement and support, a sense of a common vision and purpose and ideals, and the periodic renewal of perspectives and energies through sharing in larger groupings. This is the reason why religious orders of men and women have always stressed community, and diocesan priests too cultivate brotherhood. Married Christians need the same sort of supporting community within which to live out their own destinies. Marriage Encounter is one of the responses to this need. Besides the encounter weekend itself, there are maintenance structures so that the good achieved on the weekend can be sustained. Couples who have made the encounter continue to share their experience and resources in a community context. The Association of Couples for Marriage Enrichment (ACME) is another national organization, operating in forty states, which offers weekends and follow-up programs for the development of better marriages and larger family communities. Some parishes have developed similar programs. These broader communities for the support and enrichment of marriage serve a vital purpose in society today. Organizing and working within such structures for couple growth and better child raising is a great contribution to the building of the Kingdom.

The Emerging Parish

In the Roman Catholic Church, parish life is changing rapidly, and will continue to change. The sharp decline in the number of priests available to do parish ministry is bringing about a restructuring of ministry which was much needed anyway but probably would not have taken place without the crisis. Lay people are being asked to take increasing ministerial responsibility. Lay lectors and eucharistic ministers, lay ministers to sick and elderly shut-ins, even lay preachers on occasion are representative of the sort of change that is taking place. Married people are increasingly involved in marriage preparation and marriage counseling, areas in which priests used to operate rather exclusively. Lay people do much of the religious education. They function on parish councils and other advisory and administrative bodies, in close collaboration with their ordained leaders. A study of the history of Christian ministry shows that all of these contemporary lay activities have abundant precedents in ages past, and that experimentation has a long way to go before we outdo our lay predecessors. Such study shows the relativity of all the ministerial arrangements people have devised through the centuries, and stimulates creative thought on the question of what ministerial structures would best meet the needs of people today. For the basis of the Church's organized life is the Spirit's distribution of gifts to individuals rather than Jesus' establishment of timeless roles and clear lines of jurisdiction. Paul puts it this way:

> Now there are varieties of gifts, but the same Spirit; and there are varieties of service, but the same Lord; and there are varieties of working, but it is the same God who inspires them all in everyone. To each is given the manifestation of the Spirit for the common good. To one is given through the Spirit the utterance of wisdom, and to another the utterance of knowledge . . . to another faith . . . to another gifts of healing . . . to another the working of miracles, to another prophecy, to another the ability to distinguish between spirits, to another various kinds of tongues, to another the interpretation of tongues. All these are inspired by one and the same Spirit, who apportions to each one individually as he wills (1 Cor. 12:4-11).

The last line is instructive, that the Spirit gives these gifts where he wills. The Spirit is, of course, not confined to official channels. Nor is there any promise that he will give any given ordained individual the cluster of preaching, teaching, counseling, and administration. Yet in the Roman Catholic Church we have operated almost as if we could bank on that, giving all that responsibility to certain individuals, and overlooking or simply wasting the gifts where they turn up in unofficial others. The task of the Christian leader ought rather to be to discern the gifts of the Spirit wherever they occur in the community, to call them forth, and to put them at the service of the people. Thus one person is prophet, another theologian, another religious education coordinator, another marriage counselor, another youth minister, another minister to the dying, another parish administrator, another spiritual director, another liturgical leader. So, on the assumption that the Spirit does gift people in various ways, and that his gifts are for the common good (v. 7), it becomes incumbent on each individual to ask: What are my gifts, and how can I best use them for the good of the community? Continued progress in this direction should bring us back to some of the ministerial breadth of earlier centuries, and free us from the stagnation currently afflicting parish life in so many quarters. In this spirit, it might be hoped that we will soon see the ordination of married as well as unmarried persons, women as well as men, to fill out the richness of the priesthood.

The main point in the context of our discussion of the apostolate is that married persons might look upon the life of the local parish, their own Christian community, as another possible arena for their apostolic endeavors. That may be where their calling lies.

The Struggle for Justice

Certainly part of the mission of married Christians today is the sort of outreach they can exercise in school, office, or factory. In some ways, this is the most important area of all, at once the most difficult to influence and the most in need of the influence of Christian values. The task is not so much evangelization as it is the creation of an environment in which persons can grow as human beings and in which they work not for the destruction but for the construction of human society. This is a big order.

Too much Christian spirituality in the past has thought too small. It has concentrated on the practice of charity at home and in relationship to individuals whose paths cross our own. It has emphasized the importance of personal prayer and worship. It has urged the morality of the Ten Commandments. But it has taught all this in a highly individualistic way. And where it has spoken of Christian mission, it has had in mind chiefly the financial support of priests and sisters in mission fields and the work of direct evangelization insofar as one's circumstances offer occasion. This is all good, but it is not a total vision. The great prophetic movement of our time is the expanding cry for economic, social, and political justice. Thinking on this scale is relatively new to us, and not very congenial either.

Yet the world we live in is obviously not the place it should be. There is trouble everywhere. As a place where human beings are created for life and happiness, where people are supposed to love and care for one another and share the goods of life in peace and joy, any casual observer would have to say the world is not doing too well. The unhappy fact is that many of us work within and on behalf of structures that block life rather than promote it, that take advantage of people, deceive them, and exploit them, rather than help them or genuinely serve them. But we devote our energies to such enterprises, further their cause, take home our earnings, and let the chips fall where they may. The profit-motive is king, and the chips do fall, generally on the defenseless. Our morality has not extended so far as to make us think of these effects, though they are highly determinative of the quality of human society. In addition, our work environments themselves could hardly be called really human. They do not foster the growth of community, they dialogue poorly or not at all, and they use people strictly for what they can produce without any concern for other aspects of their life and development. That these environments are rather inhuman is attested by the fact that those who work in them want to spend as little time as possible there, come away emotionally exhausted or at least starved, and take vacations as often as their means permit.

The problem that cries out to be addressed most urgently of all is the great economic imbalance of the world. The situation was graphically portrayed a few years ago in the Alternate Christmas Catalog in these terms. If the whole world were a village of one hundred people, six of those people would possess nearly half the wealth of the village, with the other ninety-four living on the other half. Eighty of the people would be living in substandard housing, sixty of them suffering from malnutrition. The six, to protect all that they were holding against the misery of the many others, would have to devote a good portion of their energy to defense. And so it is. The people of the United States are those six people, six percent of the world's population. And they spend more per capita on defense than the average individual among the ninety-four has to live on. The world has a limited supply of oil left, and daily the six people burn up half of what is burned in the whole world. While the world starves, the six feed half of their grain crop each year to livestock, so that they can continue to consume meat at the rate they do. But it takes an average of twenty pounds of feed grain to produce one pound of chicken, pork, or beef.

There might be some inaccuracy in these figures, but they do paint a rough picture. They will probably be deeply distressing to most people of good will in the United States. As a people we have in fact always been quite generous in taking up

71

relief collections. But this is not enough. The problem needs to be addressed at its root, and the root of it is that world economics are so arranged that the rich live at the expense of the poor, and keep getting richer while the poor get poorer. If this is the case, it is not enough to skim off some of our surplus and give it back as relief. President Kennedy's AID program in the sixties purported to be a grand act of U.S. largesse toward the poor of Latin America, but the fact is that for every dollar we put into Latin America, we took two out. This is why we are not much loved there in spite of all our "generosity." A native-born Latin American priest, talking to a group of religious men and women in Berkeley who were interested in mission work in Latin America a few years ago, advised them not to go down. "Take your mission rather to your own business and government leaders," he said. "Tell them we can no longer afford to subsidize you people at the rate of several billion dollars a year."

Mahatma Gandhi used to say that anyone who takes more than he or she needs is stealing. The world situation today, with dire poverty in some quarters and superfluous abundance in others, cries out to be redressed. To change it, we will have to look at our consumption patterns, our level of living, the orientation of our business enterprises. We will have to learn to be discriminating as to where we spend and with whom we invest our money. We will have to make ourselves aware of evident instances of injustice, and join the movements which oppose them. And we will have to talk about these things until many more people see and acknowledge their injustice and begin to take similar action.

When the Second Vatican Council underscores the call of all Christians to participate in the mission of the Church, so that life and happiness might be possible not just for a few but for all, the immense economic task of righting the present imbalance is certainly one of the major apostolic tasks envisioned. The major theme of conciliar, papal, and episcopal pronouncements over the last fifteen years has been that laboring to secure justice in the world is an essential part of the preaching of the Gospel.

We have strayed some distance from theology of marriage, it seems, and are dealing with global issues. What do they have to do with marriage? They relate not so much to marriage as they do to married people and their children. Families live in and from the marketplace, and their involvement with it shapes both the marketplace and themselves. The great commandment has a particular urgency in our homes and in relation to those who are nearest. But its domain extends well beyond them. It is as large as the body of Christ. The Christian home can be a beautiful place, and our theological reflection has concentrated there. But such reflection is not complete until it surveys the broader context within which the home is situated and looks at that setting with the mind of Christ. No follower of his can close the door and let the rest of the world go by while human need cries out for relief.

And Jesus went about all the cities and villages, teaching in their synagogues and preaching the gospel of the kingdom, and healing every disease and every infirmity. When he saw the crowds, he had compassion for them, because they were harassed and helpless, like sheep without a shepherd. Then he said to his disciples, "The harvest is plentiful, but the laborers are few; pray therefore the Lord of the harvest to send out laborers into his harvest" (Mt. 9:35-38).

Suggestions for Further Reading

Vatican II, *Pastoral Constitution on the Church in the Modern World—Decree on the Apostolate of the Laity*
Synod of Bishops, *Justice in the World*

Juan Luis Segundo, *The Community Called Church*
Bernard Cooke, *Ministry to Word and Sacraments*
Karl Rahner, *The Shape of the Church to Come*
Walbert Buhlmann, *The Coming of the Third Church*
Alternate Celebrations Catalogue (Alternatives 1975, 701
N. Eugene St., Greensboro, N.C. 27401)

Chapter Eight

POSSIBLE FAILURE

We have sketched the ideal of Christian marriage and glimpsed its spiritual possibilities. It remains to say a word about its possible failure. We all know Christian couples who set out on the journey with the highest hopes and ideals, and who sooner or later find themselves face to face with apparently insurmountable obstacles. We witness the breakup of Christian marriages, and sometimes the beginning of second marriages which seem to be considerably more successful. Couples who have gone through these painful readjustments are left wondering how they stand with the Church. Are they simply out because of the breakup of their first marriage?

Laws or Ideals?

It must be remembered that Jesus deals in ideals. Most of his ideals are very high. He tells us when we are slapped by another we should turn the other cheek; that we should never take an oath, but simply always tell the truth; that we should give to anyone who asks (Mt. 5). He tells us to love our enemies, to forgive seventy times seven times, not to lust after anyone even in our hearts. He tells us to sell all we have and give to the poor (Mk. 10), to pluck out the offending eye or cut off the offending hand and throw them away (Mt. 5), to have faith strong enough to cast mountains into the sea (Mk. 11). It is plain that he shoots pretty high. He also tells married persons not to leave their spouses and marry others. He states this neither more nor less strongly, legally, nor absolutely than he states the other ideals. Let us examine the texts.

> Whoever divorces his wife and marries another commits adultery against her; and if she divorces her husband and marries another, she commits adultery (Mk.10:11-12).

> If your right eye causes you to sin, pluck it out and throw it away (Mt. 5:29).

> Everyone who looks at a woman lustfully has already committed adultery with her in his heart (Mt. 5:28).

> Do not swear at all, either by heaven, for it is the throne of God, or by the earth, for it is his footstool (Mt. 5:34).

> Whoever divorces his wife, except for unchastity, and marries another, commits adultery (Mt. 19:9).

> It is easier for a camel to go through the eye of a needle than for a rich person to enter the kingdom of God (Mk. 10:25).

> If anyone strikes you on the right cheek, turn to him the other also; and if anyone would sue you to take your coat, let him have your cloak as well (Mt. 5:39-40).

All statements are equally apodictic—except that Jesus' saying on divorce seems to admit in Matthew of an exception not conceded in Mark (unchastity), and that exception softens its absoluteness. Yet no one plucks out his or her eyes, we do swear in court even in Christian countries, we do not usually turn the other cheek to the offender or add more to the spoils of the robber, and we seem to be far less afraid of riches than we are of divorce. Could it be that in all cases except that of divorce, we have rightly understood that the statement sets us an ideal we will never fully realize, but toward which we should keep striving? Then why do we otherwise understand Jesus' ideal of Christian marriage?

Notice his pastoral practice. He is not ideally for young men leaving home with half their parents' fortune and squandering it in loose living, but in the story of the prodigal son, there is immediate forgiveness for the failure (Lk. 15). He is not ideally for adultery, but he saves the adulterous woman from the crowd and tells her he does not condemn her (Jn. 8). He does not encourage sinful women, but again immediately forgives the sinful woman who washes his feet, and praises her publicly besides for the largeness of her love (Lk. 7). He says that the person who puts his or her hand to the plow and then turns back is not fit for the Kingdom of God (Lk. 9:62), but when his own Peter denies him three times he gives him an opportunity to express his love in a threefold affirmation and the matter is finished (Jn. 21). The ideal is one thing. Pastoral treatment of flawed human beings caught up in the complexity of life is quite another. And so it must be in his Church. Jesus does not give his people laws; he sets them ideals.

Is this perhaps too facile an interpretation? Are we not dealing with a strict law here, one of the Ten Commandments: "Thou shalt not commit adultery"? Jesus says that to divorce one's spouse and marry another is adultery. Is not compromise here a clear abrogation of one of God's commandments?

Even the commandments have always admitted of exceptions in traditional Christian morality. The third commandment has been understood, at least in the Roman Catholic Church, to enjoin attendance at Mass and abstention from servile work on Sundays—except for excusing causes. The fifth commandment absolutely forbids killing—but we have always made exceptions for self-defense under attack and for just war. The seventh forbids stealing, but we have always permitted it where one's survival is at stake. The eighth forbids lying, yet we have allowed for "mental reservation" where the inquirer

77

has no right to the truth. The complexity of life, in short, simply does not allow for unexceptionable laws. And that is because in most situations of human choice, legitimate values contend with one another and it is usually impossible by any choice to honor them all. We have to choose the values which seem to be the greatest. And so, for example, in a given situation one might choose to withhold the truth from another, not for lack of regard for the truth, but for love of the inquirer or of some third party. One might work just as hard on the Lord's day as on any other, not for contempt of the Lord, but because it is the only way to support one's family. A married couple might choose contraception for a time, not because they do not respect the generative process or new life, but because in their circumstances it seems that larger values in conflict with these are better served by contraception. On the same principle, a couple caught in an impossible marriage might choose the alternative of divorce, not because they do not reverence the ideal of permanence in marriage, but because as they see their situation, more value seems to be served by the choice of divorce. Where human life is concerned, all laws except the law of love are valid only "by and large" or "for the most part." Yet laws are indispensable. They enshrine values, and keep us reminded of them. And they are valid for the most part.

Paul as Pastor

What about Paul? Is he different from Jesus or like him in his teaching and practice? Very much like him, it seems. He too sets forth what sounds like an absolute law on the indissolubility of marriage, and says he has it from the Lord.

> To the married I give charge, not I but the Lord, that the wife should not separate from her husband (but if she does let her remain single or else be reconciled to her hus-

band)—and that the husband should not divorce his wife
(1 Cor. 7:10-11).

But again in practice he allows for exceptions, notably the
exception we have come to call "the Pauline privilege." It
obtains when one of two married non-Christians becomes a
Christian, and the non-Christian partner desires to separate.

> If the unbelieving partner desires to separate, let it be so;
> in such a case the brother or sister is not bound. For God
> has called us to peace (1 Cor. 7:15).

What is very instructive here is the principle on which
Paul allows the exception: that "God has called us to peace."
Surely this principle has broader application than merely to
the case of a dispute arising from the conversion of a marriage
partner. In fact, today that particular issue would probably
cause relatively little dispute. Peace can be disrupted in a very
large number of ways, and if God calls us to peace, divorce
may be indicated in quite a variety of marital circumstances—
e.g., alcoholism, physical violence, constant nagging, domi-
nance of an extra-marital affair, total lack of communication,
the loss of all love, severe neurosis or psychosis. These are not
always grounds for divorce. But they might be. Sometimes
they do make for unbearable situations.

But perhaps Paul feels free to allow his one designated
exception because the partners were unbelievers and one remains an unbeliever, so that the marriage covenant was never
sealed by God. But notice that the saying quoted from Genesis
as a basis for the indissolubility of marriage, on the lips of
Jesus in Mark, and presumably also in the mind of Paul, goes
back not only before the Christian but even before the Jewish
era, to the primordial time of the creation itself.

> From the beginning of creation, "God made them male
> and female." "For this reason a man shall leave his father

and mother and be joined to his wife, and the two shall become one flesh." So they are no longer two but one flesh. What therefore God has joined together, let no one put asunder (Mk. 10:6-9).

In other words, it is not just Christian marriages, or even Jewish marriages, but all human marriages that are to be indissoluble, because this is simply God's creative intention for man and woman. In spite of this, Paul allows for divorce in certain circumstances, because "God has called us to peace." That is an important guide for pastoral practice, and brings Paul into perfect harmony with Jesus.

And it speaks to situations that commonly arise. For although Christian marriage should be a sign of the love with which Christ loves the Church, and husband and wife should be revelation and grace for one another and for their children and acquaintances, family situations sometimes develop in the course of time in which love is conspicuously absent, and what actually exists brings much larger doses of death than life to all concerned. The marriage is not constructive but destructive of peace, joy, freedom, and personal development. Does God want people to stick together to the bitter end in these circumstances in spite of everything? It seems not. For what possible good?

He is God not of the dead but of the living (Mk. 12:27).

I have come that they may have life, and have it more abundantly (Jn. 10:10).

The Options

What options are open to people who find themselves in a marriage that seems to have died? Let us take it a step further, and presume that one or other of them wishes to marry again and wants to do so within the Church and with full privileges of participating in the sacraments.

They might seek an official annulment of their first marriage through a Church tribunal. This is a declaration that a Christian marriage never existed in the first place, because some important condition was not met. The grounds on which such annulments are granted are considerably broader today than they were some years ago, because of a growing awareness of the importance of psychological factors such as freedom, maturity, and discretion at the moment of covenant—in short, the psychological capacity to make a lifetime commitment to another human being.

Sometimes the seeking of an annulment is quite impractical. Perhaps public testimony is difficult to obtain, one of the spouses is unwilling to cooperate, or the backlog of cases already in the courts promises a long wait. Annulment may be the wrong route anyway. Perhaps the marriage was quite sound in its inception, and all the conditions for a Christian marriage were met. Yet five, ten, twenty years down the road, the marriage is dead or has become intolerable, in the judgment of the parties involved. To seek an annulment on a legal technicality would be dishonest in this case, even if it were possible to find such a technicality. What options are open in such a circumstance as this?

There is the "internal forum" or "good conscience" solution. It presumes a person involved in a second marriage who wishes to have full sacramental communion with the Church. Such a person approaches the sacrament of reconciliation and expresses sorrow for whatever guilt there may have been in the breakup of the first marriage. Thus absolved, he or she can receive the other sacraments. Some pastors in these cases ceremonially regularize or bless the second marriage as well, once they have reasonable assurance that it is stable and bears a Christian character.

To some people this will seem too lax. It is admittedly

something of a departure from the rather rigid practice which prevailed at least in the Roman Catholic Church within living memory. Why the sudden change? On this, a couple of things need to be said.

There was point in the older practice. People involved in marital difficulties need to be cautious in the solution they take. To move quickly to divorce could be a great mistake. What human relationship is there that does not prove problematic at times, and how much real personal growth takes place, either in the individual or in the relationship, without pain and struggle? Granted all of a person's faults and failings, does not he or she still deserve and deeply need love? Many an older married couple can look back to crises like these, and, while they vividly recall the pain of them, can rejoice now in retrospect because they were the growth times. Such couples are more closely and lastingly bound together precisely because of the struggles they went through. In marriage, as in all other areas of human experience, the paschal mystery is the pattern of the coming of the Kingdom.

> Truly, truly I say to you, unless a grain of wheat falls into the earth and dies, it remains alone; but if it dies, it bears much fruit. He who loves his life loses it, and he who hates his life in this world will keep it for eternal life (Jn. 12:24-25).

Sometimes two people in difficulties do well to choose to weather the storm in hope. They will seek pastoral or psychological counseling, try to get perspective on things by talking with experienced married friends, pray and talk through their problems with each other. The Church's perennial concern for the permanence of marriage rests on the conviction that where a marriage can be saved, more of the values lie on the side of saving it than on the other side. And the Church always has in mind the ideal of Christ's faithfulness.

But, as we have seen, this will not answer every case.

Sometimes there is no hope. Sometimes everything has been tried, and tried more than once, and there is no improvement. Sometimes the attempt to discuss matters only makes matters worse, and friends and counselors themselves begin to agree that a breakup seems to be the best option. Sometimes life together is all death with no resurrection, and the kind of dying going on is not the sort that brings new life or growth, but only continual darkness and despair and the slow destruction of the personality. Such situations need to be faced. And what the official Church is realizing with growing clarity is that the parties involved must themselves take moral responsibility for their lives, and find solutions without undue dependence on official teachers or legislators. These are the factors which have led toward increasing use of the "internal forum" (as opposed to the external forum or court) or "good conscience" (personal judgment) solution to divorce and remarriage situations. Also contributing is the Church's clearer grasp of itself as a community of reconciliation. The embodiment of Christ's own Spirit of forgiveness and reconciliation in the world, the Church cannot bar its doors against those who have made a mistake or even sinfully failed in the matter of marriage. It does not do this in other matters. Nor can it coldly order people to remain single to the end after such a failure. It must help them rather to bind up their wounds and rebuild their lives.

Christianity is a religion for adults. Paul repeats over and over that Christ has freed us from the law, as well as from sin and death. Freedom is God's gift to us in Christ, and freedom he wants us to have. He does not hedge us about with legislation. The freedom he extends entails responsibility, of course. We are responsible for our lives and our choices in a way that no one else is or can be. Paul speaks to this theme often.

For freedom Christ has set us free; stand fast, therefore, and do not submit again to a yoke of slavery (Gal. 5:1).

But he cautions against self-deception.

> "All things are lawful for me," but not all things are
> helpful. "All things are lawful for me," but I will not be
> enslaved by anything (1 Cor 6:12).

> For you were called to freedom, brothers and sisters; only
> do not use your freedom as an opportunity for the flesh
> (Gal. 5:13).

Taking Christian adulthood seriously, and returning to the
New Testament ideal of Christian freedom in the Spirit, was
one of the great achievements of the Second Vatican Council.

Besides the choice of staying together and the choice of
divorce and remarriage, there is a third possibility. A person
might choose separation without remarriage. The single life
might be positively chosen for a high Christian motive, precisely in the context of the marital sacramentality we exam-
ined earlier. In the Matthean discussion of marriage, Jesus
says:

> It is not everyone who can accept this saying, but only
> those to whom it is granted. There are eunuchs born that
> way from their mother's womb, there are eunuchs made
> so by other people, and there are eunuchs who have made
> themselves that way for the kingdom of heaven. Let the
> person accept this who can (Mt. 19:12).

This text, we know, has often been invoked in support of the
celibate life of priests and religious, but its first application
seems to lie elsewhere. It occurs in a discussion of marriage
and the difficulty of remaining faithful to one's spouse in
marriage. Jesus does not back down on the ideal he has posed,
but raises it a notch higher. A person whose spouse has left
him or her might choose to keep the door to reconciliation
open by not marrying again. Such a stance of fidelity bears

witness to the kind of faithful love God has for his people even when they are not faithful to him; it remains open always to return and reconciliation in a kind of eloquent sacramentality. This is a special call, not given to everyone, as Jesus' final word makes clear. But with the help of a supporting Christian community, it is a viable option.

Marriage Preparation

The whole discussion of the possibility of failure in marriage, and the attendant pain and dislocation everyone experiences in such an eventuality, should alert us to the importance of good marriage preparation. "An ounce of prevention is worth a pound of cure," says the proverb. In Jesus' words in Luke:

> For which of you, desiring to build a tower, does not first sit down and count the cost, whether he has enough to complete it? (Lk. 14:28).

Many Christians go into marriage ill prepared. To them, the sacramental meaning of the event is simply that it begins with a church ceremony and that it lies under obligation to last till death. That is not much help. There are personal hazards too. Maturity may be lacking. There is sometimes little self-knowledge, little self-possession, and insufficient judgment to assess one's prospective spouse and the possibilities for a long-lasting relationship. Emotions can so rule the day that many of the important issues which need to be talked out in advance are touched on lightly or not at all. To have been baptized Christians once upon a time and now to be in love are scarcely sufficient warrant for entering upon one of the most serious contracts human beings can make. The statistics are sobering. Divorce is the outcome of one-third to one-half of the marriages in the United States; and the younger the couple is at the outset, the higher is the probability of divorce. Some thought needs to be given to the preliminaries.

One of the healthy developments in the changing Roman Catholic parish is that marriage preparation is increasingly in the hands of older married couples. They are chosen because of the quality of their own marriages and the experience they have accumulated. The priest makes important contributions at certain points in the process, particularly with a theology of marriage, and helps make the judgment of readiness. But married people carry the burden of the preparation because they understand more intimately the style of life, the issues that need to be discussed in advance, the sort of problems that are likely to arise and some ways of dealing with them. Even where the judgment of readiness is concerned, qualified married couples will have as good an idea as the priest does, especially if they have moderated most of the preparation.

Some of the better writing on marriage in contemporary society should furnish the basis for courses in marriage preparation. David and Vera Mace, for example, who have been active in marriage preparation and counseling for decades, point up the three most likely trouble spots in the married relationship: sex, in-laws, and finances. They also set down three requirements for a marital relationship to be able to stand the test of time: (1) a mutual commitment to growth together (2) good communication skills (3) the capacity to accept conflict positively and to resolve it creatively. Part of marriage preparation consists in facing the likely problem areas together and talking them through. There should also be some work at developing the essential communication skills, perhaps particularly learning how to deal with anger. It is very helpful too to share personal autobiographies, and to discuss the expectations each person brings to marriage. How many children do they have in mind? How important will religion be? How extensive a social life is envisaged, and what about friendships which are not shared? In particular, how will she be affected by his relationships with other women, he by hers with other men? Who will do the household chores, take care of the children, manage the budget, bring home the money? How will leisure time be typically spent? How much dependence on the other does each envisage, how much independence, how much sharing, how much space? What level of living is expected? These are not easy questions nor are they all the questions, and answers will be provisional anyway. But discussing such matters in advance could save much grief later. One hates to think of people flying into lifetime commitments without sufficient attention to matters of such consequence.

Such a searching process might well lead to the realization that the couple is not in a position to marry, at least not at the present time. This is painful, but far less painful than the same discovery after marriage is underway and the first child perhaps already in the stork's mouth. The best course may be to give the whole thing up. In other cases, to wait and see what time might do. Sometimes two people who do not seem to be in a position to marry insist on marrying anyway. Then it seems best to advise them to marry in some other way, not sacramentally, because they do not show the conditions for the kind of Christian commitment envisioned in this sacramental state. After some years, perhaps, if the marriage proves viable and a genuine religious interest still runs strong, the union could be blessed as a Christian sacrament. But what must at all costs be avoided is automatically marrying people in church just because the parents want it, or it seems more beautiful there, or the rest of the family or friends have all been married in church. There is a little more involved in marriage as Christian sacrament than returning nostalgically to a forgotten place to sing a hymn and take some pictures with a priest or minister whose name has just been learned.

Suggestions for Further Reading

Stephen Kelleher, *Divorce and Remarriage for Catholics?*
Vatican II, *Declaration on Religious Freedom*
Joseph and Lois Bird, *Marriage is for Grownups*
David Mace, *Getting Ready for Marriage*
David and Vera Mace, *How to Have a Happy Marriage*

Epilogue

We have covered some ground. And we have found perhaps some answers to the question: What light does Christian faith shed on the human institution of marriage? The light seems to be considerable. Marriage is a sacrament of the love Christ has for his Church. As such it is a high vocation, a call to follow the Lord in his worship of the Father and his self-giving love to other persons. It involves a man and woman and their children in relationships within the Body of Christ which enable them to bring his self-revelation and grace home to one another in powerful ways. It involves them in the paschal mystery of Christ's own coming to completion through a process of myriad deaths and resurrections. This experience of theirs is not for themselves alone but for other people as well, for all within their ambience and all to whom their outreach may extend. Married Christians are a leaven for the Church and for the world.

The married state, far from being a backwater in the Church for those who cannot brave the currents of real sanctification, is a superb context for growth in Christian holiness. Its demands for selflessness are constant, whether they come from one's spouse, the children, or others who come and go. Marriage is a life-project which requires a great deal of trust in the goodness and care of God in constantly changing and sometimes downright frightening circumstances. It is a setting to which God's call and invitation and even his judgment have ready access through all the human channels so closely surrounding the individual. Its dialogue is long and at various points will touch the depths, confronting us with issues we would rather not face yet which we must face if we would grow. Its apparent ordinariness is reminiscent of the sort of milieu in which Jesus found God and served him to the fullest—in the midst of the human family, in the ordinariness of everyday life, with its routine work, its many regular and irregular demands and opportunities, its simple joys and sorrows, its strivings and hopes, its creations and redemptions, its deaths and resurrections. It is at once a familiar, intensive setting, and a center for a broad circle of secondary relationships of giving and receiving.

When love begins to grow deep between two people, one thing above all is crucial: that the relationship be grounded in God. We are too small, too fragile, and too vulnerable to distortions to try to go it alone in a venture as difficult as human love. The future yawns uncertainly. We still have much to learn about ourselves, much to experience and react to, much to discover about the other. What will present itself in the way of health, financial success or failure, new relationships, we have no way of telling. What the arrival of children may bring (if they arrive), what mid-life and ageing may do, how long life will last in you or me, we do not know. In giving the gift of the self to the other for life, we scarcely know what we give; in receiving it, what we receive. One thing we know. This covenant is a bold venture and needs God as base and horizon. He is "our rock, our fortress, our deliverer, our God in whom we take refuge" (Ps. 18).

People have been known to ask too much of each other in marriage. Especially if love comes after long loneliness (and even if it does not), there is a temptation to regard the lover as deliverer and savior, and to ask him or her from this day forth

90

to be one's all. This is an impossible assignment for flesh and blood. It recalls the drowning person who grabs one around the neck and hangs on tight. Both go down together. No one can be God for us. Human love is great, but human need is deeper still. Again Augustine is there to remind us that we are made for God and nothing less will do. And again the psalmist has a line: "Only in God will my soul be at rest; from him comes my hope of salvation" (Ps. 62). However profound the lover may be, he or she remains finite reality. There is no one who can meet all our needs even at the level of human sharing. We all need a larger social circle. But even when that is in place, we still need God. Two human beings stand a much better chance of happiness if they refrain from asking one another to be God.

Finally, one of the deepest human needs of all is the need to worship. Without worship, our horizons are too small. To whom shall we give thanks when life is glorious and inexpressibly good? Whom shall we praise when the glory in the depths of things, especially in the human spirit of a good man or woman, flashes forth and nearly overwhelms us? To whom shall we turn in amazement when we experience the love of the other for us as broader, higher, and more potent than the love of that person alone, when it comes to us as transcendent assurance and transcendent blessing, mediated by a caring man or woman? At those times it will be a joy to remember that it is indeed "in him we live and move and have our being" (Acts 17:28), and that wonder and praise and thanksgiving are appropriate any hour of the day or night.

> O the depth of the riches and wisdom and knowledge of God! How unsearchable are his judgments and how inscrutable his ways! "For who has known the mind of the Lord, or who has been his counselor?" "Or who has given a gift to him that he or she should be repaid?" For from him and through him and to him are all things. To him be glory forever. Amen (Rom. 11:33-36).